D0455567

Richard Wagner's Visit to Rossini
and
An Evening at Rossini's in Beau-Sejour

Richard Wagner's Visit to Rossini (*Paris 1860*)
AND
An Evening at Rossini's in Beau-Sejour (*Passy*) 1858

by Edmond Michotte

---

translated from the French and annotated, with an introduction and appendix, by

HERBERT WEINSTOCK

Chicago

London

THE UNIVERSITY OF CHICAGO PRESS

Designed and illustrated by Warren Chappell

Library of Congress Catalog Card Number: 68–16706
The University of Chicago Press, Chicago 60637
The University of Chicago Press, Ltd., London W.C.1

Printed in the United States of America

Preface

EDMOND MICHOTTE (1830–1914), a wealthy Belgian amateur composer-pianist, achieved some notoriety by his propagandizing for (and performances on) the Mattauphone, a set of thirty-eight graduated musical glasses in a rectangular box which were tuned by increasing or decreasing the amount of water in each of them. Invented in about 1855 by Joseph Mattau of Brussels, the Mattauphone was made to sound by rubbing wet fingers around the rims of its constituent glasses. Michotte, however, was not any sort of eccentric: he was for many years President of the Administrative Council of the Conservatoire Royal de Musique at Brussels, to which he gave his large, important collection of Rossiniana, which notably includes many of Isabella Colbran Rossini's opera scores, the collection of first-printed librettos of Rossini's operas formed by the composer's father, and various memorabilia. In his Brussels palace, Michotte gave the first (private concert) performance in Belgium of Boito's *Mefistofele*. Some time after 1893, he published privately a thirty-one-page booklet entitled *Souvenirs: Une Soirée chez Rossini à Beau-Séjour (Passy) 1858*, a wonderfully vivid account of an evening at the Villa Rossini during which the sixty-six-year-old composer set forth the principles and practice of *bel canto* as that "lost art" had been understood in his youth.

More importantly, Michotte issued at Paris in 1906 (but had printed at Brussels) a fifty-three-page booklet, the cover of which is reproduced here. The present book is a textually complete translation of Michotte's two booklets, to which an Appendix adds translations of brief accounts by Eduard Hanslick (1860 and 1867) and by Emil Naumann (1867) of calls on Rossini.

Doubt naturally has been expressed about the reliability of Michotte's detailed reproduction of the conversation between Rossini and Wagner. Ernest Newman began by referring slightingly to Michotte (*The Life of Richard Wagner*, 4 vol. [New York, 1933–41], III, 12):

> It was in March 1860 that Wagner and Rossini met for the only time in their lives. In 1906 one E. * Michotte published a brochure in which he

* Surely Newman could have ascertained Michotte's given name and identity?

> *claimed* [italics mine] that he had been a member of the small circle of literary men who gathered round Wagner in Paris in 1860, that it was he who took Wagner to Rossini's house and introduced him, and that his brochure is based on notes made at the time of the conversation between the two. Wagner nowhere makes any mention of Michotte: perhaps he had forgotten his existence when he came to write *Mein Leben.*

Then, having conceded some credibility to Michotte's account because it agrees "in essence" with the accounts given by Wagner (a notoriously bad witness) in *Mein Leben* and the "Erinnerungen an Rossini" that he wrote for the Augsburg *Allgemeine Zeitung* (December 17, 1868) right after Rossini's death, Newman says, without specifications: "His little book contains many errors on points of fact; * but biographers and historians will hardly expect from any man a minutely accurate recollection of a conversation of nearly half a century before." (Michotte had not claimed to recollect the conversation; he stated that he had preserved the notes that he had taken of it in 1860.)

* Michotte erred in describing *Der Ring des Nibelungen* as then (1860) "almost finished"; in saying that in 1860 Wagner "just had finished" the scenario of *Die Meistersinger von Nürnberg;* and perhaps in calling Gustave Doré a "close friend" of Wagner—though the two men were more than merely acquainted. But it seems tendentious to call three errors "many."

Finally, Newman, convinced of Michotte's reliability for reasons that he does not advance, swings around completely: "All in all, however, when full allowance has been made for Michotte's mistakes and embroideries, there seems little reason to doubt that he was present at the interview, and that the talk was substantially as he represents it to have been." The present writer, having become familiar, during years of research into the life of Rossini, with Michotte's dignified and completely honorable character, finds no doubt possible that the Belgian was a reliable, truth-telling witness.

Ernest Newman was much more generous to Rossini than to "one E. Michotte":

> Rossini can certainly be acquitted of any ill-will towards Wagner: he was neither fool enough to be blind to the fact that there must be something in the man who could win such admiration from men of the quality of Liszt, Bülow and many others, nor base enough to see merely an occasion for witticisms in the spectacle of an idealist fighting for his very life against journalistic gangsters the real character of whom no one knew better than Rossini himself.

The fact is that thanks to Michotte's meticulous note taking and his preservation of the notes for more than forty-five years, we have an almost stenographic report of a conversation between

E. MICHOTTE

SOUVENIRS PERSONNELS

LA VISITE

DE

R. WAGNER A ROSSINI

(PARIS 1860)

DETAILS INEDITS

ET

COMMENTAIRES

(AVEC PORTRAITS)

1906

Richard Wagner

Paris G. Rossini 1860

THE PORTRAITS of Wagner and Rossini included herein are enlargements of photograph cards (that of Wagner by P. Petit, that of Rossini by Numa Blanc) which were given to me by the two masters precisely in 1860, at the time when their interview took place. Wagner, exhausted by work, was then very thin.

Rossini and Wagner in Paris in 1860, one year before the notorious production of *Tannhäuser* at the Opéra, four years before Rossini's composition of the *Petite Messe solennelle.* Michotte, who appreciated and befriended Wagner and was on terms of the closest friendship with Rossini during the last dozen years of the Italian composer's life, cannot, of course, have written down verbatim everything that the two men said while they were saying it. The booklet that he published in 1906 nonetheless performs the near miracle of bringing us, across the decay and destruction of more than a century, an approximate transcript of their conversation, thus providing not only an exposition by Wagner of his theories about the music drama but also firsthand reports by Rossini—an acute observer—of meetings with Beethoven, Weber, and Mendelssohn. *La Visite de R. Wagner à Rossini (Paris 1860)* is a unique and invaluable document.

Une Soirée chez Rossini à Beau-Sejour (Passy) 1858, less of a mother lode, is scarcely less interesting, for it brings us Rossini's own ideas about *bel canto*, singing in general, and many of the great singers of the first half of the nineteenth century. In an Appendix, I have subjoined to the two Michotte texts translations of shorter conversations with Rossini by Eduard Hanslick and Emil Naumann, both interesting in themselves and both throwing further light on Rossini's attitudes toward Wagner.

With heavy-handed irony, chance brought death to the eighty-four-year-old Michotte in the Séminaire Léon XIII at Louvain, where he had taken refuge during the burning of his chateau by German soldiers: the date was August 31, 1914.

HERBERT WEINSTOCK

NOTE TO THE READER: *Numbered footnotes are Michotte's; other footnotes and any words in square brackets have been inserted by me. Points of suspension are in Michotte's published texts: I have deleted nothing in the translation.* H. W.

CONTENTS

(MICHOTTE'S DEDICATORY LETTER)

TO

*A. Gevaert**

MY GOOD FRIEND, you will recall the concert that R. Wagner organized at the Théâtre-Italien [Salle Ventadour] in Paris (January 25, 1860), the concert in which, under his own direction, he permitted us to hear for the first time (I have the program here at hand):

The Overture to *Der fliegende Holländer*
The Overture and March with chorus from *Tannhäuser*

---

* François-Auguste Gevaert (1828–1908), Belgian musicologist and composer.

The Prelude and Wedding Celebration from *Lohengrin*
The Prelude to *Tristan und Isolde* *

In the musical world of that time, it was the sort of event to arouse Parisian curiosity to a fever because of the violent polemics that had been provoked in the public press by the appearance of Wagner's revolutionary writings concerning his very daring ideas about reforming the music drama.

People went in crowds to see the man, to hear his works.

You will remember the effervescence of that disturbed audience; the very strange atmosphere in the hall, where a number of partisan fanatics did not restrain themselves at all from manifesting their hostile feelings overtly; where others—poseurs as much as ignoramuses—thought it good form to attract attention to themselves by raillery and persiflage; while some listeners, truly impressed, nonetheless did not dare to express their opinion except as hedged about with multiple re-

* The audience burst into applause after the seventeenth measure of the *Tannhäuser* March, but was baffled by the *Tristan* Prelude, of which Wagner had written to Mathilde Wesendonk that it was "so incomprehensibly *new* to the musicians that I had to lead them from note to note as though prospecting for precious stones in a mine."

strictions intended to dilute the too-laudatory burden of their approval.

A very agitated group had gathered in the lobby during the interruption that preceded the second part of the program. A circle was formed around Halévy, Ambroise Thomas, Auber, Clapisson, etc.*

The *Tannhäuser* Overture was under discussion . . .

You arrived.

"And you, Gevaert," Jouvin ** exclaimed, "what do you have to say about that farce of an overture, toward which one would be showing excessive politeness if one did not swallow it as though it were the overture to a . . . farce?"

"What I'd say," you replied, "is that I wish that I had done it as a way of taking the shortest road to posterity."

"Ah! You make good jokes," Jouvin retorted.

---

* Jacques-François-Fromental-Élie Halévy (1799–1862), operatic composer (*La Juive*, etc.) and pedagogue; father-in-law of Bizet. Ambroise Thomas (1811–1896), operatic composer (*Hamlet, Mignon*, etc.) and pedagogue. Daniel-François-Esprit Auber (1782–1871), composer of operas (*Fra Diavolo, La Muette de Portici*, etc.) and operettas (*Le Cheval de bronze, Les Diamants de la couronne*, etc.). Antoine-Louis Clapisson (1808–1866), operatic composer (*La Perruche*, etc.) and violinist.

** Benoît-Jean-Baptiste Jouvin (1820–18??), musical journalist and biographer.

Then he added (in the manner of a *boulevardier*): "You know, *mon p'tit*, that doesn't take me in!"

And now, behold—that overture has taken the road to posterity. As your friend, I regret only that it was not you who composed it.

The above is in relation to the account to follow—*Wagner's Visit to Rossini*—an account that at first I had no intention of making public.

You know about it: the notes that I have preserved from my long relationship with Rossini—and in which I again find all the details of that interview with Wagner—in fact, I always have thought of them as a record of intimate confidences that up to now I never have dreamed of divulging outside a restricted circle of friends. Among those friends, it is true, some former intimates of the entourage of the composer of *Il Barbiere* [*di Siviglia*] who still survive often have urged me to put into print some extracts from these memories.

A similar desire was expressed to me last year when, at one of the Wagner family's receptions at Bayreuth, the course of the conversation having directed attention to the Master's visit to Rossini in 1860, I found myself able to furnish the most precise circumstantial account of the nature of that interview, at which I was present.

Taking into consideration those instances and

still others that occurred later, I yielded, and that is how it now happens that I exhume a document—buried for forty-six years in my boxes—the contents of which I dare to believe perhaps still offer a certain contemporary interest despite their retrospective nature.

Read this, my dear Gevaert, and let yourself be carried back to the time of our good years of youth in Paris—when, like me, you knew these two men of genius, later immortalized, whose physiognomies I shall re-trace and whose words I shall restate.

To you, then, the homage of these souvenirs.

Your affectionate,
E. Michotte

Brussels, April 15, 1906

Richard Wagner's Visit to Rossini

(*Paris* 1860)

[PARIS 1860]

VERY DIVERSE REPORTS used to be current about the visit that Wagner made to Rossini at the time (March, 1860) when the German Master was staying in Paris in the hope of staging his opera *Tannhäuser* there. With the help of imagination, that meeting was interpreted in the most fantastic way by the press and the public.

Wagner himself commented upon it much later in an article that he published in a Leipzig journal [1] on the occasion of Rossini's death. He did

[1] *Errinnerungen* [*sic*] *an Rossini* (1868) [published, not in Leipzig, but in the Augsburg *Allgemeine Zeitung* (December 17, 1868)].

so very briefly, not mentioning details, which perhaps he did not recall after eight years; or to which—possibly—he did not from his point of view attribute enough significant importance to decide to place them in evidence.

That interview, however, was so essentially typical that to leave an account of it in oblivion would be regrettable.

I shall recount later on how, by a series of circumstances, I, having been present, found myself in a position to be able to reproduce in a scrupulously exact narrative the various phases of the conversation that took place between these two famous men.[2]

---

[2] All the nonsense then invented on this subject—around which a legend was formed which survives even to this day—finally coalesced to claim:

That at first Rossini energetically refused to see Wagner . . .

That, being unable to evade the meeting any longer, he received him very rudely and showed special aggressiveness toward him . . .

That Wagner, very uneasy—pale as a corpse!—stammered forth many full excuses, repented with regard to his writings . . . etc. . . .

As many absurdities as fables.

I assert that at the time of the meeting no reporter would have had any way of knowing the smallest details of an essentially private conversation that took place unexpectedly during a courtesy call about which neither Rossini nor Wagner had any wish to satisfy public curiosity.

Also, it is to form a wrong notion of the characters of

But, at the outset, a few words to determine the positions that Rossini and Wagner occupied at that time in Paris.

It was during the winter of 1860 [March, 1860]. Wagner was living at No. 16, rue Newton (near the Barrière de l'Étoile), in a small house (later destroyed) which he had furnished mostly with his own furniture, brought from Zurich, where it had graced a residence that he had called the Azyl [*sic*]. Thence, in 1859, he had set out for France. Accustomed to those furnishings, which reminded him of a milieu that he had left regretfully, he wanted to be surrounded by various objects because constant sight of them would evoke still-vibrant memories of that wholly charming woman, that Mathilde Wesendonck for whom, during years of proximity at Zurich, he had conceived the enthusiasm about which one knows; that woman who exercised so much influence upon the direction of his genius.

---

these two great spirits to believe one of them—known for his urbanity—capable of attacking a visitor whom he had admitted to his home; and the other—who already had given more than enough proof of his indomitable courage—disposed to humble himself or stand for the least attack that would hurt his dignity.

A simple appeal to good sense suffices to destroy such assertions forever.

In that peaceful house he lived very modestly. Being near the Bois de Boulogne, he went out only to take a daily walk accompanied by a very lively dog that he loved to watch as it leaped about him. He spent the rest of the day collaborating uninterruptedly with Edmond Roche on the French translation of *Tannhäuser*.* In the intervals, he devoted himself to the tetralogy [*Der Ring des Nibelungen*], putting the final touches on the orchestration of that gigantic work, then already almost finished.**

His first wife *** lived with him and took care of the household. She was a person of bourgeois aspect, very simple, who effaced herself as much as she could.

Evenings, and particularly on Wednesdays, he received some few friends. They were about a

* The completed French translation of the *Tannhäuser* libretto was credited to three men: Roche, Richard Lindau, and "Charles Nuitter" (Charles-Louis-Étienne Truinet).

** In 1860, *Der Ring des Nibelungen* was far from being "almost finished": there remained to be completed the composition of *Siegfried* from the middle of Act III, the orchestration of that opera, and the composition and orchestration of *Götterdämmerung*.

*** Minna Planer (1809–1866), a minor actress, had become Wagner's wife in 1836. After a tempestuous married life that included more than one temporary separation, Wagner saw her for the last time in Dresden in November, 1862; she died there in January, 1866.

dozen, I believe, of those by whom he was not misjudged at that time and who went to seek him out in his solitude. I shall mention: Gasperini, Ed. Roche, Villot, Hans von Bülow, Champfleury, G. Doré, Lacombe, Stephen Heller, Émille Olivier [*sic*] and his young wife (Liszt's daughter) * . . . I was fortunate in being one of those habitués, which brought me the privilege of frequent friendly contacts with Wagner, which were consolidated later on.

Wagner, who had no connections in Paris and did not seek any, was happy to have this entourage of a few faithful friends. When the bell rang to announce an arrival, one could see with what speed

* Agénor de Gasperini (1825?–1868), musical dilettante and writer, author of *La Nouvelle Allemagne musicale: Richard Wagner* (Paris, 1866). Edmond Roche (1828–1861), poet and musician, principal translator of the *Tannhäuser* libretto into French. Frédéric Villot, *conservateur des musées impériales,* to whom the French translations of Wagner's librettos were dedicated. Hans von Bülow (1830–1894), pianist, conductor, writer, first husband of Liszt's daughter Cosima, later Wagner's second wife. Champfleury (pseudonym of Jules Husson, also called Fleury, 1821–1889), painter, sculptor, and writer; his brochure on Wagner (1860) was republished in his *Grandes Figures d'hier et d'aujourd'hui* (1861). Gustave Doré (1833–1883), painter and engraver, close friend of Rossini and admiring acquaintance of Wagner. Louis (Brouillon) Lacombe (1818–1884), composer and pianist. Stephen Heller (1813–1888), Hungarian Jewish pianist and composer. Émile Ollivier (1825–1913), politician and cabinet minister, married Liszt's daughter Blandine.

the Master, knowing that it was one of us, rushed, alert and joyful, to greet a friend.

From that moment on, he devoted himself exuberantly to abandoned chatter. Always unforeseeable, he soon charmed us by judgments marked by great loftiness of thought on subject in esthetics, history, philosophy . . . Then there were humorous sallies of astounding verve, at times even approaching prankishness.

He expressed himself readily in French; but when ideas boiled up in his mind, the impatience that he felt while trying to find the right word suggested to him word associations which were sometimes of a very original nature.

The interest of these reunions grew even greater when Hans von Bülow was one of the visitors. Then Wagner, never having to be begged, was pleased to allow us to hear—with the great pianist accompanying—not only fragments of *Tannhäuser* (with the French text), but also parts of *Tristan*, the orchestration of which was complete. A stupefying thing—Hans von Bülow sight-read at the piano the polyphonic pages of a score in which the writing is very complex. What can one say abut that intense interpretation with which the Master initiated us into the real significance, the profound character of his thought just as

he had conceived it? What fire! what animation! what exuberance of declamation! As for his voice—not always true!! for example—*the decomposed voice of a composer*, as he jokingly said—and of a sort, he added, to put to flight all mastersingers except those of Nuremberg! An allusion to *Die Meistersinger*, the scenario of which he just had completed.*

That, then was the unknown life of Wagner in Paris. Despite his dislike of paying calls, he nevertheless had been unable to dispense with the common formalities with regard to some personages

* Wagner had written a preliminary sketch of the *Meistersinger* at Marienbad in 1845. He did not redraft it until 1861—or complete the libretto until late January, 1862. The score was finished only in 1867.

of the musical world. He saw Auber, Halévy, Ambroise Thomas, etc. . . . He knew Gounod.[3]

[3] It was after those calls that, one evening among intimates, Wagner gave us his impressions of these composers. Here is a résumé:

"Halévy's operas, façade music! . . . Would you believe that I admired them sincerely in my early youth? As one is at that naïve age, I was a bit of a ninny then. The man, whom I just saw, seemed to me cold, pretentious, not very sympathetic.

"Auber—he makes music adequate to his personality, which is fundamentally Parisian, intellectual, full of good breeding, and . . . very flirtatious, as one knows. All of that is reflected in his scores. I love him as a man and esteem him highly as a musician.

"Rossini—it's true that I haven't seen him yet, but he is caricatured as a great epicurean, stuffed not with music—of which he was emptied long ago—but with mortadella! [By 1860, it was thirty-one years since Rossini had completed *Guillaume Tell,* his last opera, eighteen years since the *Stabat Mater.*]

"Gounod—an inflamed artist, in a perpetual swoon. An irresistible charmer in conversation. An affected melodist, he lacks both depth and breadth; at most, he grazes those two qualities; but always without being able to take hold of them."

Champfleury risked answering: "One should not, however, underrate the fact that in such melodious roles as Faust and Marguerite, and above all in the Garden Scene, Gounod has introduced an expressive note not previously known in French operatic music."

At the name of Faust, Wagner jumped.

"Ah, get on with you!" he exclaimed; "I've seen that theatrical parody of our German *Faust.*

"Faust and his crony Méphisto absolutely made upon me

As for Rossini, whom he had not yet met, he was in a dilemma. Knowing that I was very intimately linked to the Italian Master, he much wanted to involve me in his hesitations. Here is what motivated them: some Parisian journals that pursued Wagner and his *music of the future* relentlessly with their sarcasms, also gave themselves the malicious pleasure of spreading among the public quantities of anecdotes cut from whole cloth and often very disagreeable about the composer of *Tannhäuser.* Wanting to lend these little histories the semblance of truth, they never hesitated a bit to

---

the effect of two ridiculous Latin Quarter students trailing a girl student.

"As for the music, it's all surface sentimentality—on a level with leather . . . kidskin . . . like gloves—with rice powder, what's more, notably in that insipid Jewel Song: '*Ah! je ris* [here a pun on *riz:* rice] *de me voire si belle en ce miroir.*' "

(Wagner hummed the first measures, then added):

"That aria, look at it, in fact, the pivot of the piece; it sums up the whole psychological gamut of that ridiculous canvas.

"O Goethe!

"For Gounod, who has a real talent, but whose temperament lacks the scope for dealing with tragic subjects, I hope that he will be discerning enough in the future to choose his librettos better! In the demi-character style, he undoubtedly would be successful."

The judgment was severe; but could anything different have been sincere from the man who had just completed *Tristan und Isolde*?

give prominence to the names of well-known people, whom they saddled with the paternity of their tittle-tattle. Rossini above all, to whom witticisms (of a taste as dubious as they were apocryphal) were attributed much too often, was cut out by

nature to be monopolized—as an always well-stocked source—by these dispensers of gossip.

It was asserted that at one of the weekly dinners at which the composer of *Il Barbiere* assembled some noted guests, at the mention of *Turbot à l'allemande* on the menu, the servants placed before the guests a very appetizing sauce, of which each then took his portion. Then nothing else was served. What did not come was the turbot. Perplexed, the guests asked one another: what does one do with this sauce? Then Rossini, mischievously enjoying their embarrassment and himself gulping down the same sauce: "And so," he exclaimed, "you still are waiting for something? Enjoy this sauce; believe me, it's excellent. As for the turbot—alas! the principal dish . . . It is just . . . at the last moment the fishman forgot to bring it; don't be surprised. Isn't it the same with the music of Wagner? . . . Good sauce, but no turbot! . . . no melody."

It was also said that, another time, a visitor entered Rossini's study and surprised the Maestro, all attention, turning the pages of an enormous score . . . that of *Tannhäuser*. After further efforts, he stopped: "At last, that isn't bad!"—and he sighed. "For half an hour I've been searching . . . now I'm beginning to understand some of it!"—The score was upside down and backward! And behold, at exactly that moment, a loud fracas was heard from the next room. "Oh! oh! what's this?" Rossini went on, "that polyphony: *Corpo di Dio!* but it strongly resembles the Venusberg orchestra." Whereupon the door was opened brusquely and the valet entered to inform the

Maestro that the maid had dropped a whole platter of cutlery!

Impressed by these stories, which he believed to be true, Wagner understandably hesitated to present himself at Rossini's home. I took pains to reassure him. I made him understand that all those nonsensical stories were pure inventions with which a hostile press amused itself by spreading them to the public. I added that Rossini—whom, because of long intimacy and daily contacts, I was in a position to know better to the bottom of his character—had too elevated a mind to demean himself by sillinesses that did not even have the merit of being witty, and against which he himself never stopped protesting vehemently.[4]

I succeeded in undeceiving Wagner, assuring him that he could present himself at Rossini's without fear, that he would be received most cordially. That decided him. He expressed the wish that I accompany him and introduce him. The meeting was set for the morning two days later.

Nevertheless, I forewarned Rossini, who at once replied: "But that goes without saying; I'll

[4] In fact, Rossini just had published in the newspapers a denial on the subject of these "malicious hoaxes." He used to say that he was afraid of two things in this world: catarrhs and journalists; that the former engendered *humeurs mauvaises* [distempers] in his body, and the latter a *mauvaise humeur* [bad humor] in his mind.

receive M. Wagner with the greatest pleasure. You know my hours; come with him when you wish." Then he added: "Have you at least made it clear to him that I am an utter stranger to all the stupidities about him which have been attributed to me?"

Having sketched in, with these details, the circumstance under which Wagner then found himself in Paris, I still must complete this rapid glance by devoting the following lines to Rossini before bringing the two masters face to face.

He then occupied, in the building at the corner of the Chaussée d'Antin and the boulevard des Italiens, that apartment on the first floor [first above the street floor] well known to all Parisians.[5]

In 1856, the Maestro, who had been living in Florence, suddenly returned to Paris—that Paris which he had not seen since 1836.*

[5] It has been established that about a century earlier than the composer of *Il Barbiere*—O, coincidence!—the composer of *Le Nozze di Figaro,* Mozart, then staying in Paris, had lodged in a building that then occupied the location on which the large house mentioned above rises today. That was the home of [Friedrich Melchior, Baron von] Grimm (1778), with whom Mozart took refuge after having left the rue du Gros-Chenet, where he had lost his mother.

* In fact, Rossini, having left Paris in 1836, returned there in May, 1843 for four months of medical treatment. His final return to Paris occurred in 1855, not 1856.

Having suffered from neurasthenia for some time, he had vainly sought help from Florentine physicians, who had not succeeded in fighting the trouble. It grew progressively worse. There was serious disquiet about the illustrious invalid's reason.

Mme [Olympe Pélissier] Rossini decided that a change of milieu was required. She considered Paris, where her husband had left behind solid friendships among numerous admirers. More even than on the help of therapeutics, she counted on the joys of returning to old friends, on the attractions of a new environment—all things of a nature, she thought, to influence beneficially her husband's enfeebled and discouraged moral state.

To conquer Rossini's resistance was not easy at first; to induce him to undertake such a journey, which he would have to make by post chaise, with frequent stops to change horses and halts at all the villages in which they would have to spend the night. For Rossini obstinately refused to travel by railroad.[6] He advanced as an excuse that to be conveyed at the will of a machine was too humiliating . . . to feel oneself transported like a package. But at bottom, by a bizarrerie of his nervous system, he was frankly afraid of the railroad.

Finally he consented. After a fifteen-day journey,* he reached Paris enfeebled and looking absolutely lamentable. The condition of his nerves, already forcefully upset by his illness, had been aggravated by the jolting and sudden turns of the journey. Upon seeing him with his face ashen, ex-

[6] The only trip by rail which he ever had risked had taken place during his visit to Belgium (1836), on the line from Brussels to Antwerp, so that he could admire the masterpieces of Rubens in the city where the painter had lived. "I still tremble in all my members," he said, "each time I think about it." [For Rossini's tragicomic musical reaction to that ride, see his "Un Petit Train de plaisir," from the *Péchés de vieillesse*, published in *Quaderni Rossiniani*, II, (Pesaro, 1954), 42.]

* Actually, the Rossinis left Florence on April 26, 1855, and reached Paris about May 25.

pressionless, his speech halting, his mind shadowed, his friends were consternated. In view of those symptoms, they could not conceal the fear that incurable softening of the brain was to be dreaded.

Thanks to the devotion of eminent practitioners, medical science succeeded in a few months in conquering that alarming condition; and as his body gradually became reestablished, the comfortable surroundings that his attentive friends were able to create around the Maestro finally relighted the flame of a mind that had been feared extinguished forever. Later, a cure at Kissingen completed the recovery. The signs of a disease that had seemed incurable were dissipated completely.

In Paris from then on, the composer of *Guillaume Tell* and *Il Barbiere* acquired an aura of glory and prestige which no one else in the musical domain equaled. His receptions became famous. The most renowned artists intrigued for the favor of having him near them. When his salons were opened, one saw the most illustrious people from all Parisian circles jostling one another there.

Amid that intellectual royalty, enveloped in an Olympian calm brought about by age, Rossini remained simple, good, affable, disdainful of arrogance, an enemy to all ostentation. And may I be permitted, in that regard, to make a *tabula rasa* of his very exaggerated reputation as a *jester* and his very undeserved one as a *scoffer*, which the Parisian journals of the time delighted to bestow upon him, attributing to him with incredible irresponsibility numerous retorts of more or less dubious taste which he never had imagined and that irreverent facetiousness toward others of which he was incapable.* He suffered from that bitter publicity, which often passed the boundaries of mischief and became frankly perfidious at his expense. He often complained, and then someone would reply: "You know, Maestro, one lends only to the rich." "To tell the truth," he would sigh, "I'd like better a little more *poverty* and a little less *generosity*. In the process of wanting to give to me, they overload, they obstruct me! And what gifts, good Lord!—garbage that splashes onto me even more than it hits the other! That exaperates me: *ma così va il mondo*."

In these few lines I have wanted to describe the very different positions occupied in Paris at that time by the two men who were about to meet. The one adulated like a demigod; the other lacking any prestige, even scoffed at, almost like a wrongdoer. And nonetheless, let us not forget, Wagner at the apogee of his genius—as great in his own eyes as he

* Here, protesting in a good cause, Michotte protested too much.

later showed himself to be to the generality—already had created the titanic work that slept there—ignored and colossal—in a corner of the modest quarters in the rue Newton: *Tristan und Isolde* entirely complete and the tetralogy of the *Nibelungen* on the point of being completed.*

As we had agreed, Wagner, keeping the rendezvous (which he had taken the superfluous care to recall to me again by letter very early that morning) came to call for me at my home. That was a few steps from Rossini's home, and we discussed him as soon as we were on the way.

When we were going up the stairs, I said to Wagner: "If Rossini is in a good mood, you will be charmed by his conversation. This will be a treat. Don't be surprised if you see me taking some notes during your interview . . ."

"For the newspapers?" Wagner asked.

"Not at all," I told him, "just for my personal souvenirs. If the Maestro were to gather the smallest notion that I could give material to the press, he would scarcely open his mouth. But then, he has full confidence in my discretion, whereas he hates any publicity at all about his private life."

* In fact, only part of *Siegfried* and none of *Götterdämmerung* had been composed. *Der Ring des Nibelungen* was completed only on November 21, 1874.

Assigning almost complete use of the apartment to his wife, Rossini had reserved for himself next to the dining room a corner with four windows looking onto the boulevard and consisting of a den that he never entered and a bedroom that he never left. A bed, a writing table, a secretary, and a small upright Pleyel piano made up the entire furnishing of this room, which was of extreme simplicity. There he unvaryingly received all callers, from the most modest of favor seekers to excellencies, highnesses, and crowned heads. There, also, he received Wagner.

When we were announced, the Maestro was just finishing his lunch. We waited for several minutes in the grand salon.

There Wagner's glance immediately lighted upon a portrait of Rossini in which he was represented half-length, life-size, wrapped in a long green mantle and with his head covered by a red cap—a portrait that has been reproduced in gravure and later became well known.

"That intelligent physiognomy, that ironic mouth—it was surely the composer of *Il Barbiere*," Wagner said to me. "That portrait must date from the period in which that opera was composed?"

"Four years later," I told him; "this portrait, painted by Mayer at Naples, dates from 1820."

"He was a good-looking youth, and in that land of Vesuvius, where women are easily ignited, he must have caused lots of ravages," Wagner answered, smiling.

"Who knows?" I said—"if he had had a valet as devoted to bookkeeping as Don Giovanni's Leporello, mightn't he perhaps have surpassed the number *mil e tre* set down in the notebook?" *

"Oh, how you exaggerate!" Wagner answered. "*Mil* I'll agree to, but *tre* more—that's really too many."

At this moment, the *valet de chambre* came to tell us that Rossini was awaiting us.

As soon as we entered, "Ah! *monsieur Wagner*," he said, "like a new Orpheus, you don't fear to enter this redoubtable precinct . . ." And, without giving Wagner time to reply: "I know that they have thoroughly blackened me in your mind . . .[7]

* Leporello, reading to Donna Elvira from his copious notebok the number of Don Giovanni's female conquests, says that in Spain they numbered "*mil e tre*" (one thousand and three).

[7] In reporting the conversation between the two masters, I have tried to reproduce it integrally as much as possible. It is quasi-verbatim, in particular as far as Rossini is concerned, he having married as his second wife Olympe Pélissier, a *parisienne*, and being accustomed to speak French, of which he knew all the fine points, argot included. As for

"With regard to you, they load me with many quips that, what is more, nothing could justify on my part. And why do *I* suffer from this fate? I am neither Mozart nor Beethoven. Nor do I pretend to be a wise man; but I do hold to being polite and refraining from insulting a musician who, like you—for this is what I have been told—is trying to extend the limits of our art. Those great devils who take pleasure in busying themselves with me should at least grant that, though I lack other merits, I do have some common sense.

"As for slighting your music, I should have to be familiar with it first; to know it, I should have to hear it in the theater, as only in the theater, and not by the mere reading of a score, is it possible to bring equitable judgment to bear on music intended for the stage. The only composition of yours which I know is the March from *Tannhäuser*. I heard it often at Kissingen when I was taking the cure there three years ago. It made a great effect, and—I assure you sincerely—as for me, I thought it very beautiful.

"And now that—I hope—all misunderstanding between us has been dissipated, tell me how you

Wagner, less familiar with this language, he frequently multiplied circumlocutions in the attempt to express his thought precisely. I have thought it my duty at times to sum up in more literary language what he said.

are finding your stay in Paris. I know that you are in discussions about staging your opera *Tannhäuser*? . . ."

Wagner seemed impressed by that welcoming preamble, spoken in a simple tone full of great good

nature. "Allow me," he responded, "illustrious *Maître*, to thank you for these friendly words. They touch me deeply. They show me how much, in the welcome that you want to accord me, your character—which I never have doubted—displays nobility and greatness. Believe, above all, I beg you, that even if you criticize me sharply, I shall take no offense. I know that my writings are of a sort to give birth to wrong interpretations. Faced with the exposition of a huge system of new ideas, the best-intentioned judges can mistake their significance. That comes about because I am late in being

able to make a logical and complete demonstration of my tendencies by performances, as complete and nearly perfect as possible, of my operas."

ROSSINI: "That is fair: for deeds are worth more than words!"

WAGNER: "And, to begin with, all my efforts at this moment are toward getting *Tannhäuser* performed. I recently played it for Carvalho,* who was favorably impressed and seemed disposed to attempt the adventure; but nothing has been decided yet. Unhappily, the ill will that has raged against me in the press for so long threatens to take the form of a real cabal . . . It is to be feared that Carvalho may fall under its influence . . ."

At the word "cabal," ROSSINI (animatedly): "What composer," he interjected, "has not felt them, to begin with the great Gluck himself? As for me, I was not spared—far from it. On the evening of the *première* of *Il Barbiere*, when, as was customary then in Italy for *opera buffa*, I played the clavicembalo in the orchestra to accompany the recitatives, I had to protect myself from a really riotous attitude on the part of the audience. I thought that they were going to assassinate me.

"Here in Paris, where I came for the first time in 1824,** having been summoned by the direction of the Théâtre-Italien, I was greeted by the sobriquet 'Monsieur Vacarmini' [Mr. Uproar], which I still have. And it's not a thing of the past, I assure you, for me to be abused in the camp of some

* Léon Carvaille, called Carvalho (1825–1897), stage director of the Opéra, Paris, and husband of the noted soprano Marie Miolan-Carvalho.

** Rossini actually reached Paris for the first time in November, 1823.

musicians and press critics leagued in a common accord—an accord as perfect as it is major! *

"It was no different in Vienna when I arrived there in 1822 to mount my opera *Zelmira.* [Carl Maria von] Weber himself—who, what is more, had been fulminating against me in articles for a long time—pursued me relentlessly after the performances of my operas at the Italian court theater. . ."

WAGNER: "Weber, oh! I know he was very intolerant. He became intractable above all when it was a question of defending German art. That could be forgiven him; so that—and this is understandable—you did not have friendly relations

* A pun on the French *accord,* which means both "accord" or "harmony" and "chord."

with him during your stay in Vienna? A great genius, and so prematurely dead!"

ROSSINI: "A great genius certainly, and a true one he was; for, being creative and strong within himself, he imitated no one. In fact, I didn't meet him in Vienna; but, you see, as a result of those circumstances I saw him later in Paris, where he stopped off a few days before starting for England. Immediately after his arrival, he paid the customary calls on leading musicians—Cherubini, Hérold, Boieldieu. Not having foreseen his visit, I must admit that when I found myself unexpectedly facing that composer of genius, I felt an emotion not too unlike the one that I had felt earlier upon finding myself in the presence of Beethoven. Very pallid, breathless from having climbed my stairs (for he was already very ill), as soon as he saw me the poor fellow thought it necessary to tell me—with an embarrassment that his difficulty in finding French words increased even more—that he had been very hard on me in his critical articles on music . . . but . . . I didn't let him finish . . . 'Look,' I told him, 'let's not discuss that. To begin with,' I added, 'those articles—I've never read them; I don't know German . . . the only words of your language, which is devilish for a musician, which I was able, after heroic application, to remember and pronounce were *ich bin zufrieden* [I am delighted].' These remarks made Weber smile, and that immediately gave him more assurance and put him at his ease.[8]

[8] Here, on this subject, a very amusing encounter that I shall let Rossini himself recount:

"During one of my walks in the Vienna streets, I witnessed a scuffle between two Bohemians, one of whom fell to the sidewalk after receiving a violent dagger thrust.

"Suddenly, the collecting of a huge crowd, from which I was about to escape when I was accosted by a police agent who was very agitated and said a few German words to me which I didn't understand.

"I answered him very politely: *ich bin zufrieden;* suddenly, questions, the violence of which appeared to me to be going *crescendo* to the point at which, faced by that armed man, I uttered my *zufriedens diminuendo,* constantly more and more polite and respectful.

"Suddenly, red with fury, he summoned a second agent, and the two of them, foaming at the mouth, seized me firmly.

"Luck had it that while they were dragging me along, the Russian ambassador passed near us in his carriage. I saw his head as he recognized me thus flanked by two policemen.

"He had his carriage stopped and asked my guardians what was happening. After some explanations in German, those bravos let me go, not without many bows and excuses, the eloquence of which I grasped only because I saw their despairing gestures.

"The ambassador had me get into his carriage, where he told me that the police agent had, at the outset, simply asked me my name so that in case of need my testimony could be sought with regard to the crime that had been committed under my eyes. (Given that the agent, after all, was merely doing his duty, my innumerable *zufriedens* had exasperated him so much that he had taken me for a practical joker of a

" 'Furthermore,' I continued, 'you have done me too much honor by discussing my operas, I who am such a small matter alongside the great geniuses of your country. And I want to ask you to let me embrace you; and believe me that if my friendship has any value in your eyes, I offer it to you completely and with all my heart.' I embraced him effusively and saw a tear appear in his eyes."

WAGNER: "He was already suffering, I know, from the consumption that was to carry him off a short time later.

ROSSINI: "Exactly. To me he appeared to be in a pitiable state: with livid coloring, emaciated, racked by the consumptive's dry cough . . . limping, too. It pained one to see him. He came back to see me a few days later, to ask for some introductions for London, as he was about to go there. I was appalled by the idea of seeing him undertake such a journey. I tried very energetically to dissuade him, telling him that he would be committing a crime . . . suicide! It did no good. 'I know,' he answered, 'my life will end there . . . But I must do it. I must

---

sinister sort and had wanted to have the commissioner himself order me to respect the police.)

"The ambassador himself having said that I was to be excused because I did not understand German . . .

" 'This man? Not at all,' the agent had replied, 'he speaks the purest Viennese.'

" 'Be polite, then . . . and in pure Viennese at that.' "

go to stage *Oberon;* my contract obliges me to; I must, I must . . .'

"Among other letters that I gave him for London—where I had formed some important relationships during my stay in England—was a letter of presentation to King George [IV], who, being very gracious to artists, had been especially affable with me. With a broken heart, I embraced that great genius for the last time with the foreboding that I should never see him again. That was only too true. *Povero Weber!* *

". . . But we were discussing cabals," Rossini went on. "This is my opinion on that subject: one can do nothing about them except fight them with silence and inertia; that is more effective, believe me, than replies and anger. Ill will is legion; anyone who wants to argue or—if you like it better—to fight with that sow never will strike the last blow. For my part, I spat on such attacks—the more they buffeted me, the more I replied with *roulades;* I fought sobriquets with my *triplets,* satires with my *pizzicati;* and all the hurly-burly stirred up by those who didn't like them never, I swear to you, was able to make me give them one less blow on the big drum in my *crescendos* or to prevent me, when

* Weber died in London during the night of July 5–6, 1826, aged thirty-nine, less than three months after the Covent Garden *première* of *Oberon.*

it suited me, from horrifying them with one more *felicità* in my finales. Believe me, the fact that you see me wearing a wig does not mean that those *b . . . utors*[9] succeeded in making me lose a single hair from my head."

Dumbfounded at first by this ultra-picturesque tirade, in which the Italian Maestro—until then solemn and reflective—had revealed himself suddenly under such a different aspect (Rossini in fact simply had returned to his natural, habitually jocular, humorous way of giving things their real names), Wagner could scarcely keep from laughing. "Oh, as for that," he answered (with a gesture toward his head), —"Thanks to what you had there, Maestro, that inertia of which you speak, wasn't it rather a real power; a power recognized by the public, and so sovereign that really one should have pitied the fools who risked opposing it? . . . But didn't I understand you to say a moment ago that you knew Beethoven?"

ROSSINI: "That's correct; at Vienna, precisely at the time I've just been telling you about, in 1822,

[9] When, during the course of the conversation, his mind brought up some memory or some natural difficulty that excited him, he thought little about framing his thought in academic language, but gave free voice to vocables of which it will be sufficient, I think, for me to underline the first letter; the rest will be divined.

when my opera *Zelmira* was presented there. I had heard quartets by Beethoven in Milan—I need not tell you with what a feeling of admiration! I also knew some of his piano works. In Vienna I attended for the first time a performance of one of his symphonies, the '*Eroica*.' That music bowled me over. I had only one thought: to meet that great genius, to see him, even if only once. I sounded out Salieri on the subject, knowing that he was on good terms with Beethoven."

WAGNER: "Salieri the composer of *Les Danaïdes?*" *

* Antonio Salieri (1750–1825) had studied with Gluck. When his opera *Les Danaïdes* was given its *première* at the Paris Opéra on April 26, 1784, it was billed as a collaboration by Gluck and himself. After its twelfth successful performance, however, Gluck issued a public statement that it had been composed entirely by Salieri. Its libretto—by François-Louis Gaud Lebland du Roullet and Louis-Théodore de Tschuddy—was partly an adaptation and partly a translation of *Ipermestra*, a text written for Gluck in 1778 by Raniero de' Calzabigi (though Gluck earlier—1744—had composed an *Ipermestra* to a libretto by Metastasio). After the first success of *Les Danaïdes*, Calzabigi sent the *Mercure de France* (August 21, 1784) a protest against its libretto's abuse of his auctorial rights. *Les Danaïdes* long remained a popular opera. At Trouville in 1855, Ferdinand Hiller mentioned Salieri to Rossini, who called him "that nice old gentleman" and added: "At that time he had a passion for composing canons. He came to our house for dessert almost every day. . . . We—my wife [Isabella Colbran], [Giovanni] David, and [Andrea] Nozzari, who usually dined with us—constituted quite a passable vocal

ROSSINI: "Exactly. In Vienna, where he had lived for a long time, he had attracted a lot of attention as the result of the vogue of several of his operas that were given at the Italian Theater; in fact, he told me that he sometimes saw Beethoven, but warned me that because of his [Beethoven's] distrustful and fantastic character, what I was asking for could not be arranged easily. Incidentally, Salieri had enjoyed equally good relations with Mozart. After the latter's death, it was suggested—and even seriously charged—that out of professional jealousy he had killed him by means of a slow poison . . ."

WAGNER: "That rumor still was current in Vienna in my time."

ROSSINI: "One day I amused myself by saying to Salieri as a joke: 'It's a lucky thing for Beethoven that, out of an instinct for self-preservation, he avoids having you at meals; for you might well send him wandering in the other world, as you did

quartet. Finally those never-ending canons made us quite dizzy, and we asked him to restrain himself a bit." Hiller remarked that Salieri's opera *Axur, re d'Ormus,* was among his earliest memories, and Rossini commented: "Like all his operas, it contains some excellent numbers. Though in *La Grotta di Trofonio* he certainly was surpassed by the poet: [Giovanni Battista] Casti's libretto is a real masterpiece. Poor Salieri! They blamed Mozart's death on him" (from Hiller's *Plaudereien mit Rossini,* vol. 2 of his *Aus dem Tonleben unserer Zeit* [Leipzig, 1868]).

Mozart.' 'Do I have the air of a poisoner, then?' Salieri replied. 'O, no!' I answered, 'you have more the air of a real craven! [*l'air d'un fieffé* c . . . ouard!]—which, in fact, he was. That poor devil, what is more, seemed to have little taste for passing as Mozart's assassin. What he couldn't swallow was that a Viennese journalist, a defender of German music—who liked Italian opera very little, and Salieri least of all—had written that 'unlike the *Danaïdes,* Salieri has emptied his cask in earnest and yet without much effort, never having had much in it.' Salieri's consternation over that was heartrending. Further, I must add, he could think of no better way of satisfying my desire than that of approaching [Giuseppe] Carpani,* the Italian poet, who

* Giuseppe Carpani (1752–1825), writer and editor, was a friend of Haydn, Mozart, and Beethoven. His monograph on Haydn (*Le Haydine, ovvero Lettere su la vita e le opere del celebre Giuseppe Haydn,* [Milan, 1812]) was plagiarized by Henri Beyle under his alternative pseudonym, Bombet (Paris, 1814). Carpani attacked the plagiarism in the pamphlet *Lettere dell'autore delle Haydine* (Vienna, 1815), which did not prevent Beyle from reprinting his plagiarism in 1817 under his more usual pseudonym, Stendhal (*Vies de Haydn, Mozart et Métastase*). Carpani was also the author of the libretto for Ferdinando Paër's popular opera *Camilla, ossia Il Sotterraneo* (Vienna, 1799) and of two pamphlets about Rossini: *Le Rossiniane, ossia Lettere musico-teatrali* (Padua, 1824) and *Lettera del Professore Giuseppe Carpani sulla musica di Gioacchino Rossini . . .* (Rome, 1826). Beethoven's arietta *In questa tomba oscura* is a setting of lines by Carpani.

was *persona grata* with Beethoven, and through whose intervention he felt sure of success. In fact, Carpani was so persistent with Beethoven that he extracted from him his consent to receive me.[10]

"Need I tell you? As I went up the stairs leading to the poor lodgings in which the great man lived, I had some difficulty in containing my emotion. When the door was opened, I found myself in a sort of hovel, so dirty as to testify to frightening disorder. I remember above all that the ceiling, which was immediately under the roof, was cracked, showing large crevices through which the rain must have come in waves.[11]

[10] Earlier, Rossini had told me that before he succeeded in seeing Beethoven through Carpani's intervention he had presented himself at the great composer's quarters spontaneously in the company of Artaria, the important publisher, who had been charged with introducing Rossini because he had constant relations with Beethoven. Rossini waited in the street; then Artaria came to tell him that Beethoven, being very unwell as the result of a cold that had affected his eyes, was not receiving anyone. It was probably this circumstance that led [Anton Felix] Schindler, Beethoven's biographer [*Biographie Ludwig van Beethovens*, 1840], to assert that he had refused to receive a visit from the Italian maestro. That day's situation had changed a few days later.

[11] This is perhaps the place to remark on some exaggeration in Rossini's account. Beethoven was then occupying with his nephew an agreeable enough apartment on the first floor of a house located in the Phargasse, in the Lehngrube neighborhood. The principal staircase, rather dark, opened onto a somewhat hidden ramshackle staircase, it is true,

"The Beethoven portraits that we know render the whole of his physiognomy faithfully

---

which led to a small room on the second floor which the great composer had made into his workroom. Rossini was taken into that room, which in fact could have led him to think that he was in a garret mansard. (I have these details directly from Ferdinand Hiller, who, during a stay in Vienna shortly after Beethoven's death, often visited that same apartment, then occupied by a tenant whom Hiller knew intimately.) But that Beethoven's misery was extreme at that time is undeniable; his biographers show us that. He lived from day to day on borrowed money, which he tried to obtain on all sides; for the sale of his manuscripts brought him nothing: thirty to forty ducats at most for a piano sonata!

enough. But what no burin would know how to express is the undefinable sadness spread across all his features, so that from under heavy eyebrows there shone, as if from the depths of caverns, two eyes which, though small, seemed to pierce you. The voice was soft and slightly fogged.*

"When we first entered, he paid no attention to us, but for some moments remained bent over a piece of printed music, which he was finishing correcting. Then, raising his head, he said to me brusquely in Italian that was comprehensible enough: 'Ah! Rossini, you are the composer of *Il Barbiere di Siviglia*? I congratulate you; it is an excellent *opera buffa;* I read it with pleasure, and it delights me. It will be played as long as Italian opera exists. Never try to do anything but *opera buffa;* wanting to succeed in another genre would be trying to force your destiny.'

"Carpani, who was with me (you must understand that he wrote out the words, and in German, there being no other way to pursue the conversation with Beethoven, whose words Carpani translated for me one after the other), interrupted

* Rossini is describing the fifty-one-year-old Beethoven of 1822, the year during which he labored ahead on the *Missa solemnis* (completed in 1823) and composed the C minor Piano Sonata, Opus 111.

immediately: 'But Maestro Rossini already has composed a large number of *opera seria* scores: *Tancredi, Otello, Mosè;* I sent them to you not long ago and suggested that you examine them.'

" 'In fact I have looked through them,' Beethoven replied. 'But look, *opera seria*—that's not the Italians' nature. They don't have enough musical science to deal with true drama; and how could they acquire it in Italy?' "

WAGNER: "That blow from the lion—it wouldn't have lightened Salieri's consternation if he had been there."

ROSSINI: "No, it certainly would not have! I told him about it later. He bit his lips . . . without hurting himself too much, I suppose, for, as I was about to tell you, he was timorous to the point at which I'm certain that in the otherworld the King of Hell, so as not to blush over the job of roasting such a coward, has had to have him sent elsewhere to be smoked! But to get back to Beethoven. 'In *opera buffa*,' he went on, 'nobody would have the wit to match you, you Italians. Your language and your vivacity of temperament destine you for it. Look at Cimarosa: how superior the comic part of his operas is to all the rest! It's the same with Pergolesi. You Italians, you make a great thing of his religious music, I know. I agree that there is very touching feeling in his *Stabat;* but its form lacks variety . . . the effect is monotonous; whereas *La Serva padrona*—' "

WAGNER (interrupting): "We must agree, Maestro (he said), that happily you refrained from taking Beethoven's advice . . ."

ROSSINI: "To tell you the truth, I really felt more aptitude for *opera buffa.* I preferred to treat comic rather than serious subjects. But I never had much choice among librettos, which were imposed upon me by the impresarios. I can't tell you how many times it happened that at first I received only part of the scenario, an act at a time, for which I had to compose the music without knowing what followed or the end of the subject. To think of it . . . what I had to do was earn a living for my father, my mother, and my grandmother! Going from town to town like a nomad, I wrote three, four operas a year. And don't think for a moment that all that earned me the means to act the *grand seigneur.* For *Il Barbiere* I received 1,200 francs, paid all at once, plus a hazel-colored suit with gold buttons which my impresario gave me so that I would be in a state to appear decently in the orchestra. That suit, it is true, may have been worth one hundred francs. Total: 1,300 francs. It had taken me only thirteen days to write that score. Taking everything into account, that came to a hundred francs per day. You see (Rossini added, smiling) that all the same I earned a big salary! I was very boastful to my father, who had earned only two francs fifty per day when he had the job of trumpet player at Pesaro."

WAGNER: "Thirteen days! That fact surely is unique. But, Maestro, I wonder how, under such conditions, shackled to that *vie de bohème* which you described, you were able to write those pages of *Otello*, of *Mosè*, superior pages that bear the mark, not of improvisation, but of thought-out labor after a concentration of all your mental forces!"

"Oh (Rossini interrupted) *I had facility and lots of instinct.*[12] Having to get along without a

[12] *J'avais de la facilité* . . . Most chroniclers, struck by this reply, which Wagner himself has reported, have thought to see in it some malicious intention, a spurt of malice imagined by the Monkey of Pesaro [*Singe de Pesaro*, burlesquing the sobriquet *cygne*—swan—*de Pesaro*] (as Rossini sometimes called himself) so as to have fun with the German master by persuading him to take this avowal at face value. . . . Nothing could be less exact; the same is true of the attitude attributed to Wagner by other publicists, that of having prostrated himself humbly before Rossini—confessing an outright *mea culpa* with regard to his doctrines.

The answer in question, I assert, was led up to quite naturally in the course of the conversation—as we just have seen—and could not leave any doubt behind as to its sincerity.

Furthermore, it is *true*. It is identical to the declaration really thorough musical education—and where, furthermore, *could* I have acquired it in Italy during my time?—I found in German scores the little that I know. An amateur at Bologna had some of them: *Die Schöpfung, Le Nozze di Figaro, Die Zauberflöte* . . . He lent them to me, and because at the age of fifteen I didn't have the means to import them from Germany, I copied them out tenaciously. I must tell you that I usually transcribed only the vocal part at first, without looking at the orchestral accompaniment. Then, on a separate sheet, I imagined an accompaniment of my own, which I later compared with Haydn's or Mozart's; after that I completed my copy by adding theirs. That system of working taught me more than all the courses at the Bologna Liceo. Ah! I feel that if I had been able to take my scholastic studies in your country I should have been able to produce something better than what is known of mine!"

WAGNER: "Surely not better—to cite only the *Scène des ténèbres* in your *Moïse*, the conspiracy in *Guillaume Tell*, or, of another sort, the *Quando Corpus morietur*. . ." *

that the Maestro was in the habit of making to his close friends when he talked to them about himself and his works.

* Wagner mentions the introductory chorus of *Moïse et Pharaon*, "*Dieu puissant du joug de l'impie*," dealing with the plague of shadows; the Act IV scene in *Guillaume Tell* in which, following Arnold's "*Amis, amis, secondez ma*

ROSSINI: "I'll have to concede that you have mentioned some happy episodes of my career. But what is all that alongside the work of Mozart, of a Haydn? I don't know how to tell you strongly enough how much I admire those masters for that supple science, that certainty which is so natural to

them in the art of composing. I have always envied them that; but it must be learned on the school benches, and one must also be a Mozart to know how to profit by it. As for Bach—not to leave your country—he is an overwhelming genius. If Beethoven is a prodigy of humanity, Bach is a miracle of God! I subscribed to the great publication of his

vengeance," those present conspire against Gessler; and a renowned section of the *Stabat Mater*.

works.* Look, you'll see it there, on my table, the last volume to appear. Can I tell you? The day when the next one arrives, that too will be an incomparably happy day for me. How I should like to hear a complete performance of his great [*Matthäus*] Passion before leaving this earth! But that's not to be dreamed of here among the French."

WAGNER: "It was Mendelssohn who first allowed the Germans to know the Passion, through the masterly performance that he himself conducted in Berlin."

ROSSINI: "Mendelssohn! O, what a sympathetic nature! I recall with pleasure the good hours that I spent in his company at Frankfurt in 1836. I found myself in that city on the occasion of a marriage that was being celebrated in the Rothschild family, and to which (I was living in Paris then) I had been invited. Ferdinand Hiller introduced me to Mendelssohn. How charmed I was to hear him play on the piano, among other things, some of his delicious *Lieder ohne Worte*! Then he played me some Weber. Then I asked him for Bach, plenty of Bach. Hiller had told me beforehand that no one interpreted [Bach] as well as he did. At first, Men-

* The Bach Gesellschaft, founded in 1850, was issuing what was intended to be a complete critical edition of Bach's music.

delssohn seemed stupefied by my request. 'How,' he asked, 'does it happen that you, an Italian, love German music so much?' 'I don't love any other kind,' I answered; then I added, in a somewhat too offhanded way: 'As for Italian music, I don't give a damn for it!' He looked at me in perplexity, which didn't prevent him from playing admirably and

with rare good nature several fugues and other pieces by the great Bach. I heard from Hiller that after we parted, Mendelssohn, recalling my sally, said to him: 'This Rossini, is he really serious? In any case, he's a very odd fish.' "

WAGNER (laughing heartily): "Maestro, I can understand Mendelssohn's stupefaction; but will you allow me to ask you how your visit to Beethoven ended?"

ROSSINI: "Oh, it was short. You understand that one whole side of the conversation had to be written out. I told him of all my admiration for his genius, all my gratitude for his having allowed me an opportunity to express it to him.

"He replied with a profound sigh and exactly these words: '*Oh! un infelice!*' After a pause he asked me for some details about the Italian opera houses, about famous singers, whether or not Mozart's operas were performed frequently, if I was satisfied with the Italian troupe at Vienna.

"Then, wishing me a good performance and success for *Zelmira*, he got up, led us to the door, and said to me again: 'Above all, make a lot of *Barbers*.'

"Going down that ramshackle staircase, I felt such a painful impression of my visit to that great man—thinking of that destitution, that privation—that I couldn't hold back my tears. 'Ah!' Carpani said, 'that's the way he wants it. He is a misanthrope, morose, and doesn't know how to hold on to a single friendship.'

"That very evening I attended a gala dinner given by Prince [Klemens von] Metternich. Still completely upset by that visit, by that lugubrious '*Un infelice!*' which remained in my ears, I couldn't, I assure you, protect myself against a feeling of inner confusion at seeing, by comparison, myself treated with such regard by that brilliant Viennese assemblage; that led me to say stoutly and without any discretion at all what I thought about the conduct of the Court and the aristocracy toward the greatest genius of the epoch, who needed so little and was abandoned to such distress. They gave me the very reply that I had received from Carpani. I demanded to know, however, if Beethoven's deafness didn't deserve the greatest pity, if it was really charitable to bring up again the weaknesses for which they were reproaching him, to seek reasons for refusing to go to his assistance. I added that it would be so easy, by drawing up a very small subscription, to assure him an income large enough to place him beyond all need for the rest of his life. That proposal didn't win the support of a single person.[13]

"After dinner, the evening ended with a reception that brought to Metternich's salons the greatest names in Vienna society. There was also a

[13] This indifference—almost criminal—which Viennese society persisted in vis-à-vis Beethoven and the precarious situation weighing upon him, is the more inexplicable in view of the fact that at this time the Master's published works had reached the number 111 in the catalogue, and therefore included the symphonies 1 through 7, *Fidelio*, quartets, trios, almost all of the works for piano, etc. And we must add that on their appearance, all these masterpieces, far from being misprized, enjoyed universal admiration.

concert. One of Beethoven's most recently published trios figured on the program—always he, he everywhere, as was said of Napoleon. The new masterpiece was listed to religiously and won a splendid success. Hearing it amid all that worldly magnificence, I told myself sadly that perhaps at that moment the great man was completing—in the isolation of the hovel in which he lived—some work of high inspiration which was destined, like his earlier works, to initiate into beauties of a sublime order that same brilliant aristocracy from which he was being excluded, and which, amid all its pleasures, was not at all disquieted by the misery of the man who supplied it with those pleasures.

"Not having succeeded in my attempts to create an annual income for Beethoven, I didn't lose courage immediately. I wanted to try to get together sufficient funds to buy him a place to live. I did succeed in obtaining some promises to subscribe; but even when I added my own, the final result was very mediocre. So I had to abandon that second project. Generally I got this answer: 'You don't know Beethoven well. The day after he became the owner of a house, he would sell it again. He never would know how to adjust himself to a fixed abode; for he feels the need to change his quarters every six months and his servant every six weeks.' Was that a way to get rid of me?

"But that's enough, I think, about me and the others who are the Past [*Passé*], even the Dead [*Trépassé*]. Let's talk about the Present and, if you'll permit it, *monsieur Wagner*, above all about the *Future*, as in any discussion your name always appears to be inseparable from that epithet. This, be it understood, without the least malicious intention on my part.—And, to begin with, tell me, are you planning to stay in Paris? As for your opera *Tannhäuser*, I'm sure that you will succeed in having it produced. There has been too much talk about that work for the Parisians to be able to stifle their curiosity about hearing it. Is the translation finished?"

WAGNER: "It is not finished yet; I am working on it actively with a collaborator who is very able and, above all, extremely patient. This is a question—for perfect understanding of the musical expression—of identifying, to put it this way, each French word with the corresponding sense of the German word, and under the same notation. It is hard work and very difficult to accomplish."

ROSSINI: "But why, in the manner of Gluck, Spontini, Meyerbeer, don't you start from the beginning by writing an opera with all the numbers adapted to a French libretto? * Wouldn't you then

* This was, of course, the procedure that Rossini himself had followed when transforming the Italian *Maometto II*

be in a position to take into consideration the taste predominating here and the special atmosphere of theatrical matters inherent in the French spirit?"

WAGNER: "In my case, Maestro, I don't think that that could be done. After *Tannhäuser*, I wrote *Lohengrin*, then *Tristan und Isolde*. These three operas, from both the literary and the musical points of view, represent a logical development in my conception of the definitive and absolute form of the lyric drama. My style has undergone the inevitable effects of that gradation. And if it is true that now I sense the possibility of writing other works in the style of *Tristan*, I swear that I am incapable of taking up my *Tannhäuser* manner again. Well, then, if I were in the position of having to compose an opera for Paris on a French text, I could not and should not follow any other road than the one that has led me to the composition of *Tristan*.

"Further, such a work as that, comprising such a disturbance of the traditional forms of opera, certainly would remain unappreciated and would have no chance, under present conditions of being accepted by the French."

ROSSINI: "And tell me, what in your mind has been the point of departure for these reforms?"

(1820) into the French *Le Siège de Corinthe* (1826), *Mosè in Egitto* (1818) into *Moïse et Pharaon* (1827).

WAGNER: "Their system was not developed all at once. My doubts go back to my first attempts, which did not satisfy me; and it was rather in the poetic conception than in the musical conception that the germ of these reforms suddenly entered my mind. My first works, in fact, had above all a literary objective. Later, preoccupied with means to use for enlarging the significance by the very penetrating addition of musical expression, I deplored the way in which the independence with which my thought was moving in the visionary realm was decreased by the demands imposed by routine in the forms of the musical drama.[14]

"Those bravura *arias*, those insipid duets fatally manufactured on the same model, and how many other hors d'oeuvre that interrupt the stage action without reason! then the *septets*! for in every respectable opera it was necessary to have a solemn septet in which the characters of the drama, setting the meaning of their roles aside, formed a line across the front of the stage—all reconciled!—to come to a common accord * (of often what accords, good Lord!) so as to supply the public with one of those stale banalities . . ."

ROSSINI (interrupting): "And do you know

[14] One should not lose sight of the fact that Wagner was born in 1813.

* See translator's footnote, page 33.

what we called that in Italy in my time? *The row of artichokes.* I assure you that I was perfectly aware of the silliness of the thing. It always gave me the impression of a line of porters who had come to sing in order to earn a tip. But what would you have had me do? It was the custom—a conces-

sion that one had to make to the public, which otherwise would have thrown sliced potatoes at us . . . or even ones that hadn't been sliced!"

WAGNER (continuing without paying much attention to Rossini's interruption): "And as for the orchestra, those routine accompaniments . . . colorless . . . obstinately repeating the same formulas without taking into account the diversity of the characters and situations. . . . in a word, all that concert music, foreign to the action, without any reason for being there except the *convention*—music that obstructs the most famous operas in many places . . . all that seemed to me something contrary to good sense and incompatible with the high mission of an art noble and worthy of that name."

ROSSINI: "Among other things, you just referred to the bravura arias. Well, what do you suppose? That was my nightmare. To satisfy at the same time the prima donna, the first tenor, the first bass! . . . those jolly fellows existed—without forgetting, above all, the qualifying *terrible feminine*—who thought it wise to count the number of measures in one of their arias, then come to me to declare that they wouldn't sing because another of their colleagues had an aria containing several measures more, not to mention a larger number of trills, of ornaments . . ."

WAGNER (gaily): "It was measured by a ruler! nothing was left for the composer to do but take a musical *meter* as collaborator for his inspirations."

ROSSINI: "Let's just call it an aria-meter! Really, when I think of those people, they were wild animals. There you have the only people who, having made my head sweat, soon made me bald. But let's leave that and go on with your reasoning . . .

"In effect, and without replying, it seems to me to deal with the rational, rapid, and regular development of the dramatic action. Only—that independence claimed by the literary conception, how to maintain it in alliance with that of musical form, which is nothing but *convention?*—you yourself used the word! For if one must obey the sense of complete logic, it goes without saying that when speaking, one does not sing; an angry man, a conspirator, a jealous man does not sing! (humorously): An exception, perhaps, for lovers, whom, in a strict sense, one can have *coo* . . . But, even more forceful: does one go to one's death singing? *Convention* in the opera, then, from beginning to end. And the instrumentation itself? . . . Who, then, when an orchestra is unleashed, could pinpoint the difference in the description of a storm, a riot, a fire? . . . always convention!"

WAGNER: "Clearly, Maestro, *convention*—and in very large supply—is imposed upon one, for otherwise one would have to do away completely with the lyric drama and even the comedy in music. It is none the less indisputable, however, that this convention, having been raised to the level of a form of art, must be understood in a way to avoid excesses leading to the absurd, the ridiculous. And there you have the abuse against which I am reacting. But they have wanted to muddy my thought. Don't they represent me as an arrogant man . . . denigrating Mozart?"

ROSSINI (with a touch of humor): "*Mozart, l'angelo della musica* . . . But who, short of sacrilege, would dare to touch him?"

WAGNER: "I have been accused, as if it were a mere trifle, of repudiating all existing operatic music—with rare exceptions, such as Gluck and Weber. They refuse, clearly with closed minds, to want to understand my writings. And in what a way! But, far from denying or not myself feeling, even to the highest degree, the charm—*as pure music*—of lots of admirable pages in justly famous operas, it is against the role of that music when it is condemned to be used as a purely diverting hors d'oeuvre, or where, a slave to routine and foreign to the stage action, it is not addressed systematically to anything but the ear's sensuality—it is against that role that I rise up and want to react.

"In my view, an opera, being destined by its complex essence to have as its aim that of forming an organism concentrating the perfect union of all the arts that contribute to making it—the poetic art, the musical art, the decorative and plastic art—isn't this a disparagement of the musician's mission, this desire to confine him to being the simple instrumental illustrator of just any libretto, which imposes upon him in advance a summary number of arias, duets, scenes, ensembles . . . in a word, of *pieces* (pieces—that is to say, things cut up in the true sense of the word) which he must translate into notes almost like a colorist filling in proofs printed in black? Certainly there are many examples of composers inspired by a moving dramatic situation who have written immortal pages. But how many other pages of their scores are diminished or nullified because of the vicious system I am pointing out! Well, as long as these follies persist, as long as one does not sense the prevalence of complete reciprocal penetration by music and poem or that *double conception* based, from the beginning, upon a single thought, the true music drama does not exist."

ROSSINI: "That is to say, if I understand you correctly, that in order to realize your ideal, the composer must be his own librettist? That seems to me, for many reasons, to be an insurmountable condition."

WAGNER (very animated): "And why? What reason is there against having composers, while they are learning counterpoint, study literature at the same time, search history, read legends? Which would lead them instinctively thereafter to attach themselves to a subject, poetic or tragic, related to their own temperament? . . . And then, if they lack ability or experience for arranging the dramatic intrigue, wouldn't they then have the resource of going to some practiced dramatist with whom they could identify themselves in a steadily maintained collaboration?

"Furthermore, there have been few dramatic composers, I think, who have not at times instinctively displayed remarkable literary and poetic aptitudes: rearranging or refashioning to their own taste either the text or the arrangement of a given scene which they have felt differently and understood better than their librettists. Not to go farther afield, you yourself, Maestro—let us take, for example, the scene of the oath swearing in *Guillaume*

Tell—would you say that you followed servilely, word by word, the text given you by your collaborators? I don't believe it. It is not difficult, when one looks at that closely, to discover in many places effects of declamation and of gradation which bear such an imprint of *musicality* (if I may say it that way), of *spontaneous inspiration*, that I refuse to attribute their genesis exclusively to the intervention of the textual scheme that was before your eyes. A librettist, whatever his ability, cannot know—above all, in scenes complicated by ensembles—how to conceive the arrangement that will suit the composer when he is creating the musical fresco as his imagination will suggest it."

ROSSINI: "What you say is true. That scene, in fact, was profoundly modified to my specifications, and not without trouble. I composed *Guillaume Tell* at the country home of my friend Aguado,* where I was spending the summer. There my librettists were not at hand. But Armand Marrast and [Adolphe] Crémieux ** (parenthetically, *two future conspirators* against the government of

* Alejandro María Aguado, Marqués de las Marismas, a naturalized Frenchman of Spanish birth, was a man of great wealth and a very generous patron of Rossini.

** Armand Marrast, writer and publicist, was a political figure of some importance who served as mayor of Paris and president of the National Assembly. Adolphe Crémieux was an outstanding lawyer and politician.

Louis-Philippe), who were also staying at Aguado's in the country, came to my assistance with changes in the text and the versification which I needed in order to work out, as I had to, the plan of *my own conspirators* against Gessler."

WAGNER: "There, Maestro, you have an implicit confession that already confirms in part what I have just been saying; it would be enough to enlarge that principle to establish that my ideas are not so contradictory, so impossible to realize, as they may seem at first.

"I assert that it is logically inevitable that, by an entirely natural evolution, perhaps a slow one—there will be born, not that *music of the future* which they insist upon attributing to me the pretension of wanting to give birth to all by myself, but the *future of the music drama*, in which the general movement will play a part and from which will arise an orientation—as fecund as it will be new—in the concept of *composers, singers*, and *public*."

ROSSINI: "In short, it is a radical revolution! And do you think that the *singers*—let's talk about them right away—habituated to displaying their talent in virtuosity, which will be replaced—if I divine clearly—by a sort of *declamatory recitative*, do you think that the *public*, habituated to—let's use the word—the *vieux jeu*, will finally submit to changes so destructive of the entire past? I doubt it strongly."

WAGNER: "There will certainly be a slow education to achieve, but it will be achieved. As for the public, does it shape the masters, or do the masters shape the public? Another situation in which I see you as an illustrious demonstration.

"Wasn't it, in fact, your very personal manner that made people in Italy forget all your predecessors; that acquired for you with unheard of rapidity an unexampled popularity? Well, Maestro, your influence, once it had passed the frontier, didn't it become universal?

"As for the singers, whose resistance you raised to me as an objection, they will have to submit, to accept a situation that, what is more, will elevate them. When they have understood that the lyric drama in its new form will furnish them, not, it is true, with the elements of easy success owing either to the strength of their lungs or to the advantages of a charming voice—they will understand that nevertheless the art demands a much higher mission from them. Forced to stop isolating themselves inside the personal limitations of their role, they will identify themselves with both the philosophic and the esthetic spirit dominating the work. They will live, if I may express myself this way, in an atmosphere in which—*everything con-*

tributing to the whole—nothing should remain secondary. Further, broken of the habit of ephemeral success through fleeting virtuosity, delivered from the torment of having to expend their voices on insipid words lined up in banal rhymes—they will understand how it will have become possible for them to be able to surround their names with a more glorious and durable aureole when they will be incarnating the characters they represent by complete penetration—from the psychological and human point of view—of their *raison d'être* in the drama; when they will base themselves on deepened studies of the ideas, customs, character of the period in which the action occurs; when they will join irreproachable diction to the prestige of masterly declamation, full of truth and nobility."

ROSSINI: "From the point of view of *pure art*, those are unquestionably long views, seductive perspectives. But from the point of view of musical form in particular, it is, as I said, the fatal blow to declamatory melody—*the funeral oration of melody*! Otherwise, how ally expressive notation, to say it that way, of each syllable of the language to the melodic form, in which precise rhythms and symmetrical concord among the constituent elements must establish the physiognomy?"

WAGNER: "Certainly, Maestro, such a system if applied and pushed with such rigor would be intolerable. But here, if you want to understand me clearly: far from brushing melody aside, on the contrary, I demand it, and *copiously*. Isn't melody the vitality of every musical organism? Without melody, nothing is or could be. Only, let us understand one another: I require it not to be that melody which, shut up inside the narrow limitations of conventional procedures, submits to the yoke of symmetrical periods, persistent rhymes, foreseen harmonic progressions, obligatory cadences. I want melody *free, independent,* unfettered. A melody particularizing by its own characteristic contour not only each character in such a way that he cannot be confused with another, but also each event, each episode inherent in the context of the drama. A melody of very precise form which, while conforming to the sense of the poetic text by its multiple inflections, can extend itself, contract itself, prolong itself [15] according to the conditions required by the musical effect that the composer wants to obtain. And as for that sort of melody, Maestro, you stereotyped a sublime specimen in the scene of *Guillaume Tell, 'Sois immobile,'* where

[15] "A melody in the battle [*mélodie de combat*]," Rossini added quickly. But Wagner, carried away by what he was saying, paid no attention to that really droll interruption. I pointed it out to him later. "For a *charge*," he exclaimed, "and behold, at least one that is led in a good corner of the mind. Ah! I'll remember that: *mélodie de combat* . . . A lucky hit!"

the very freedom of the singing line, accentuating each word and sustained by the breathing strokes of the violoncellos, reached the highest summits of lyric expression."

ROSSINI: "So I made *music of the future* without knowing it?"

WAGNER: "There, Maestro, you made music of all times, and that is the best."

ROSSINI: "I'll tell you that the feeling that moved me most during my life was the love that I felt for my mother and my father, and which they repaid me at usurious rates, I am happy to tell you.

It was there, I think, that I found the tone that I needed for the scene of the *apple*—in *Guillaume Tell.**

"But one more question, *monsieur Wagner,* if you'll permit me: how to fit into this system the simultaneous employment of two, or several, voices, as well as that of choruses? Should one, so as to be logical, forbid them? . . ."

WAGNER: "In fact, it would be rigorously logical to model musical dialogue on spoken dialogue, assigning speech to the characters one after the other. But on the other hand, one also admits that, for example, two different people can find themselves in the same spiritual state at a given moment—sharing a common feeling and, as a result, joining their voices to identify themselves in a single thought. In the same way, several assembled characters, if there is a discussion involving diverse feelings animating them, can sensibly use the means of expressing them simultaneously while each one determines individually what is his own.

"And do you understand now, Maestro, what immense resources, infinite, are offered to composers by this system of applying to each personage of

* In the finale of Act III of *Guillaume Tell,* before shooting the apple from his son's head, Tell orders the boy to kneel and pray motionlessly ("*Sois immobile, et vers la terre incline un genou suppliant*").

the drama, to each situation—a typical melodic formula susceptible—while preserving its original character—of lending itself to the most varying, the most extended developments during the course of the action? . . .

"Further, these ensembles, in which each of the characters appears in his own individuality, but in which these elements are combined in a polyphony appropriate to the action—these ensembles no longer will present the spectacle, I repeat, of those absurd ensembles in which characters animated by the most contradictory passions find themselves, at a given moment, condemned without rhyme or reason to unite their voices in a sort of *largo d'apothéose*, in which the patriarchal harmonies make one think only 'that one cannot be better than in the bosom of his family.' [16]

"As for choruses," Wagner continued, "this is a psychological truth: that the collective masses obey a determined sensation more energetically than the isolated man—such as dread, fury, pity . . . Then it is logical to admit that the crowd can express such a state collectively in the sound-language of the opera without shocking good sense. Further still, the intervention of choruses, granted

[16] An allusion to the very popular finale ["*On ne saurait être mieux qu'au sein de sa famille*"] of *Lucile,* an opera by Grétry.

that it be indicated logically in the situations of the drama, is a power without equal and one of the most precious agents of theatrical effect. Among a hundred examples, shall I recall the impression of anguish in the vivid chorus in *Idomeneo*—'*Corriamo, fuggiamo!*'—not to forget, either, Maestro, the admirable fresco in your *Moïse—the so desolate chorus of the shades*? . . ."

ROSSINI: "Again! (striking his forehead, and very amusingly), decidedly, then, I had—me too—some disposition toward the *music of the future?* . . . You are salving my wounds! If I were not too old, I'd start over, and then . . . let the *ancien régime* beware!"

"Ah, Maestro—Wagner replied at once—if you had not laid down your pen after *Guillaume Tell* at thirty-seven years—a crime! you yourself have no idea of everything that you could have extracted from that brain there! At that time, you had done no more than begin . . ."

ROSSINI (again becoming serious): "What should I have done? I had no children. Had I had any, I doubtless would have continued to work. But, to tell you the truth, after having worked and composed forty operas during fifteen years of that so lazy period, I felt a need to rest and I returned to Bologna to live in peace.*

* In January, 1866, Rossini—then nearly seventy-four and looking back thirty-seven years to his abandonment of opera

"Also, the condition of the Italian theaters, which already during my career left much to be desired, then was in full decay; the art of singing had darkened. That was to be foreseen."

WAGNER: "To what do you attribute such an unexpected phenomenon in a country in which beautiful voices are superabundant?"

ROSSINI: "To the disappearance of the *castrati*. One can form no notion of the charm of voice and consummate virtuosity—which, lacking something else, and by a charitable compensation—those best of the best possessed. They were also incomparable teachers. The teaching of singing in the master schools attached to the churches and supported at the churches' expense generally was confided to them. Some of those schools were famous. They were real singing academies. The pupils flocked to them, and some of them abandoned the choir loft to devote themselves to theatrical careers. But after

—was to write to Giovanni Pacini: "Dear Giovanni, be at peace; keep in mind my philosophic intention to abandon my Italian career in 1822, my French in 1829; this foresightedness is not given to all; God accorded it to me, and I always bless him." It had not, of course, been that simple, and elsewhere in the same letter, as if still feeling some need to justify to others his retirement from operatic composition, Rossini speaks of music as "this art which has as its only basis the ideal and feeling," adding that it could not be separated from "the influence of the times in which we live. Today, the ideal and feeling are directed exclusively toward *steam*, *rapine*, and the barricades. . . ."

a new political regime was installed throughout Italy by my restless contemporaries, the master schools were suppressed, being replaced by some *conservatories* in which, though good traditions existed, absolutely nothing of *bel canto* was conserved.

"As to the *castrati*, they vanished, and the usage disappeared in the creation of new customs. That was the cause of the irretrievable decay of the art of singing. When it had disappeared, *opera buffa* (the best that we had) was cast adrift. And *opera seria?* Audiences, who even in my time showed themselves not very likely to rise to the height of that great art, showed no interest in that sort of spectacle. The announcement of an *opera seria* on the posters usually resulted in attracting some plethoric spectators wanting to breathe in a cooling aria * remote from the crowd. There you have the reasons—and there were others too—why I judged that I had something better to do, which was to keep silent. I committed suicide, and *così finita la comedia* [*sic*]."

Rossini rose, clasped Wagner's hands affectionately, and added: "My dear *monsieur Wagner*, I don't know how to thank you enough for your call, and particularly for the exposition of

* A pun on the Italian word *aria*, which means both air and one sort of vocal solo.

your ideas, so clear and so interesting, which you have been kind enough to give me. I who no longer compose, being at the age at which, rather, one *decomposes* while waiting to be *re-decomposed* truly—I am too old to being looking toward new horizons; but your ideas—whatever your detractors may say—are of a sort to make the young reflect. Of all the art, music, because of its ideal essence, is the one most exposed to transformations. They are without limits. After Mozart, could one have foreseen Beethoven? After Gluck, Weber? And the end certainly is not after them. Each one must strive, if not to advance, at least to discover the new without worrying about the legend of a certain Hercules, a great traveler toward the visible, who reached a certain spot at which he could no longer see very clearly and, it is said, set up a column and then retraced his steps."

WAGNER: "Was it perhaps a private hunting stake, to prevent others from going farther on?"

ROSSINI: "*Chi lo sa?* Doubtless you are right, for one is assured that he displayed a brave predilection for hunting lions. Let us hope, however, that our art never will be limited by a placer of that sort of column. For my part, I belonged to my time. To others, in particular to you whom I see vigorous and impregnated with such masterly tendencies, falls the creation of what is new and comes next—which I wish you with all my heart."

Thus ended that memorable interview, during which, for the long half hour that it lasted, these two men—in whom the intellectual verve of the one did not leave in peace the humorous repartee of the other—never, as I can attest, showed the slightest sign of being bored.

Rossini, while conducting us back through the dining room next to his chamber, suddenly stopped in front of a delightful small piece of furniture in fine marqueterie placed between the two windows and familiar to all habitués of his salons. It was a small mechanical organ of the seventeenth century, of Florentine manufacture.

"Look"—the Maestro said to Wagner—"this little organ is going to let you hear some old airs from my country which may perhaps interest you." He touched the spring, and at once the instrument supplied, in old-time flageolet sound, its whole repertoire. That consisted of short popular airs.

"What do you think of it?"—Rossini asked—"there is some of the past, even of the dead. It is simple and naïve. Who was the unknown composer? Some fiddler, it would seem. It dates from long ago unquestionably, and it still lives! Will as much remain of us in a century?"

Of us! Certain hair splitters have not failed to use the chance to see here, in this remark to Wagner, a sharp thrust disguised under the semblance of senile bonhomie. That was not, I think, the Maestro's intention. That reflection—which, what is more, was identical to remarks that I had heard him make in the same reference on other occasions, was spoken simply, without *arrière-pensée*, apparently on the spur of the moment.[17] Wagner paid no attention to it.

Then we bade farewell to the Maestro.

---

[17] This recalls to me that one evening after dinner, the Maestro, having done the honors of the little organ for Auber, said to him: "*Voilà!* If in fifty years some similar mechanism still sounds forth my '*Di tanti palpiti*' [in *Tancredi*], that, I am sure, will be all that will remain of me." AUBER: "And your *Barbiere*? Do you believe that it won't be played in a century, and in all the centuries?" ROSSINI: "Before half a century has passed, all of our music probably will be Chinese, as the political high hats assure us that the Asiatic peril is already approaching the antechamber of Europe. You undoubtedly will still be living (Auber was almost ninety), seeing that you are determined to *conserve* yourself in order, I suppose, to justify your title as Director of the *Conservatory;* then you will have the satisfaction of hearing your *Cheval de bronze* in Chinese, after which celestial and piquant Mandarins certainly will rejuvenate your fiber by provoking new and perhaps heroic variations as an epilogue to those in *Les Diamants de la couronne*." AUBER: "As for the Chinese, I adore the little feet, but not so much that this . . ." ROSSINI: "As a musician you are mistaken, for these damsels don't know how to regulate their steps except by means of *appoggiature*." AUBER: "Redoubled steps [*des pas redoublés*] to the Chinese maidens, then!" And so forth.

Going down the stairs, Wagner said to me: "I swear to you that I did not expect to find in Rossini the man who appeared before me. He is simple, natural, serious, and shows himself quick to take an interest in all the points that I touched upon during this short talk. I couldn't set forth in a few words all the ideas that I develop in my writing about the conception that I have formed of the necessary evolution of the lyric drama toward new destinies. I have had to restrict myself to some general views, making use of practical details only when that could make my point immediately. But, be that as it may, it was to be expected that my assertions would seem excessive to him, given the systematic spirit that prevailed when he made his career and with which he necessarily remains deeply imbued today. Like Mozart, he possessed melodic inventiveness to the highest degree. Further, that was marvelously seconded by his instinct for the stage and for dramatic expression. What mightn't he have produced if he had been given a strong, complete musical education? especially if, less Italian and less skeptical, he had felt inside him the religion of his art? There can be no doubt that he would have taken off on a flight that would have raised him to the highest peaks. In a word, he is a genius who was led astray by not having been well prepared and not having found the milieu for which his high creative abilities had designed him. But I must declare: of all the musicians whom I have met in Paris, *he alone is truly great.*"

Having left Wagner and gone home immediately, I hastened to put into order the notes that I had taken during the conversation of these two celebrated men.

I now make this comment: that Rossini, who had regaled us so emotionally with his visit to Beethoven while expressing all the admiration that he felt for that colossal genius, was far from doubting that he had a colossus of the same stamp before him.

Wagner, let us not forget, had not yet conquered the prestige that celebrity confers. His name, though it already was spreading across Germany after performances of *Tannhäuser* and *Lohengrin* in various theaters, had—it is true—acquired notoriety in Paris; but it was the polemicist rather than the musician who was in view in the numerous usually hostile articles that the press was multiplying against him. From that resulted the fact that in the eyes of Rossini—who was not familiar with any of Wagner's music—Wagner, in short, then occupied as a personality a position much below that of a Gounod, a Félicien

David *—perhaps represented, rather, the type of Teuton who intoxicates himself on the suggestions of an exalted brain, more talker than musician, too radical in his renovating utopias for anyone to believe seriously in the possibility of their realization. At first, therefore, Rossini had listened to Wagner with the appearance of polite curiosity rather than with the marks of lively, concentrated interest. During the course of the talk, Rossini's impression was modified, his perspicacity being well known, and he was not long in perceiving that this Teuton was *a brain*.

Furthermore, that meeting between these two men of genius, of whom the one, sated with fame, had survived the most brilliant of careers for thirty years; of whom the other, on the eve of an incomparable glory, had not yet revealed to his contemporaries everything that his titanic faculties concealed; that interview was what it should have been: courtly and simple on the part of Rossini, dignified and full of deference on the part of Wagner.

The latter, when presenting himself before the Pesaro master, had no illusions, as goes without

* Félicien David (1810–1876) had become famous in Paris in 1844 with his symphonic ode *Le Désert*, which was played at the Salle Ventadour for an entire month, and in 1851 with his opera *La Perle du Brésil.*

saying, about the welcome that a setting-forth of his doctrines would receive. He did not even expect that Rossini would put so much urbanity into prolonging their talk; and the cry of alarm: *but it is the funeral oration of melody which you pronounce there*, did not at all surprise him. It was the *cri du coeur* that he could not have failed to foresee. Also, it was not with the intention of being understood that Wagner had asked for the interview; but above all in the hope of being able to study psychologically at close range this strange musician, miraculously endowed, who, after so astonishingly swift a rise in the development of his creative faculties—from which *Guillaume Tell* finally emerged—then, at the age of thirty-seven, had had nothing more urgent [to do] than to separate himself from his genie as one disembarrasses oneself of an encumbering burden, in order to bury himself in the bourgeois *farniente* of a colorless life without worrying more about his art than if he never had practiced it. That was the phenomenon that attracted Wagner's curiosity, and which he wanted to be able to analyze.

Also, it could only please him to seize the occasion to protest in person against the absurdities that an ignorant and aggressive press attributed to him on the subject of his purported feelings of disdain for the operatic music of the most illustrious masters, his predecessors, with Mozart at the head, Meyerbeer and Rossini following. To this last—as we have just seen—he made [the denial] in dignified and precise terms, restricting himself to a simple denial, as was fitting for a man who did not have to free himself of imputations spread abroad by malice or of allegations that his declarations were consciously false.

Furthermore, absolved when, in the presence of the Italian master, he set forth his ideas in their real significance, he did not embarrass himself with either oratorical precautions or ambiguous subterfuges; even less did he dream of mitigating them by means of restrictions smelling of court holy water while he was categorically formulating his criticism of the defective, worm-eaten secular organism of the opera and the vicious system that composers employed to ornament their music. It must be agreed that this arrow was only slightly blunted as shot directly toward Rossini.

The latter, as we have seen, was far from taking umbrage; he talked courteously in the sprightly, humorous tone habitual with him. But, noticing the change that little by little came over his attitude, one clearly perceived, I repeat, that he had not been slow to understand the real value of his visitor. Rather than a visionary bursting with self-sufficience and rambling on in the confused phraseology of incoherent pedantry—which Rossini's entourage had pictured this German as being—he soon understood that he had before him an intelligence of the first order, robust, clear, conscious of its strength, capable of taking an eagle's eye view of the unlimited spaces of the art of music and resolved to raise itself into their highest reaches.

All equivocation having been dissipated quickly, the meeting of these two men, then, had led to a reciprocal feeling of esteem which persisted thereafter with as much sincerity as deference. And yet, how disparate these two geniuses!

Wagner utterly Germanic in temperament, absolute, imperious, combative, nourished by the school of Schopenhauer, as profound and sublime as Beethoven, a brain perpetually at the boil, dominated and tormented by his *Genius*, his *Demon*, as he called it; conscious of his apostolate, which was his strength, and conscious of his duty to create, which was his destiny.

The other, Rossini, the Italian, an alert spirit, brilliant, adept in the philosophy of Epicurus, enjoying the surfaces of things rather than taking the trouble to penetrate deeply: letting himself live from day to day while tossing improvisations to all the winds, having as a *Genius*, in lieu of Wagner's ravaging *Demon,* a sweet and generous fairy full of caresses; not succumbing to the allurements of his art except when constrained to, and then appealing to the complaisance of a marvelous instinct always ready to respond to his solicitations.

Such was the contrast between these two musicians, of whom the one, in the course of a tempestuous life, had to fight to the end, to create up to his last breath; of whom the other, having completed the first period of an existence crowded with triumphs and delights, rested from the seventh luster of his age, satisfied with himself and his work, just as the Eternal rested on the seventh day of the Creation.

So I put my notes in order, and that same evening, as usual, went to Rossini's, where one always was sure to meet some interesting people. There I found, among others, AZEVEDO,* a music critic attached to the paper *L'Opinion nationale*, a fanatic Rossinist and one of Wagner's most violent persecutors.

Seeing him, Rossini addressed him banteringly: "Eh, Azevedo, well! I saw him, he came . . . the monster . . . your *bête noire* . . . Wagner!"

While the Maestro then went on to talk with Carafa,** Azevedo took me aside to obtain some details about that interview. But Rossini came up and interrupted us an instant later. "You talked in vain"—he went on, addressing Azevedo—"this Wagner—I must confess—seems to me to be en-

* Alexis-Jacob Azevedo (1813–1875), long familiar to readers of *Le Ménestrel*, Paris, wrote for its publisher what was for many years the standard Rossini biography: *G. Rossini: Sa Vie et ses œuvres* (Paris, 1864).

** Michele Enrico Carafa, Principe di Colobrano (1787–1872), was a prolific composer of operas and lifetime friend of Rossini, whom he assisted in the completion of both *Mosè in Egitto* and *Adelaide di Borgogna*, and for whom he prepared the Paris Opéra version (1860) of *Semiramide*.

dowed with first-class faculties. His whole physique—his chin most of all—reveals an iron-willed temperament. It's a great thing to know how to *will.* If he possesses the gift of *being able* in the same degree, as I believe he does, he will get himself talked about."

Azevedo fell silent; but he whispered in my ear: "Why is Rossini addressing the *future?* Zounds! This animal now does nothing but talk too much about him in the *present.*"

As for Rossini, he certainly could not suspect the degree to which, ten years later, when he would be no more, his prediction would be not only fulfilled but prodigiously exceeded.

Is it not a very extraordinary detail to remember about the composer of *Il Barbiere* and *Guillaume Tell*—that he had known, forty years apart, two vast geniuses, of whom the one, Beethoven, at the beginning of the century, revolutionized instrumental music—and of whom the other, Wagner, toward the end of the same era, was to revolutionize opera—while during that interval of waiting between *Fidelio* and *Tannhäuser,* it devolved upon him, the Italian, to fascinate his contemporaries by the melodious charm of new forms, of which he was the brilliant initiator, and to add his undeniable portion of influence to the future destinies of the musical drama?

I said above that the two masters never met again.

After the failure of *Tannhäuser* at the Paris Opéra,* French and some German journals published at Wagner's expense new stories, again attributed to Rossini. Then some maladroit friends intervened—one asks with what aim?—to present the Italian Maestro's attitude to Wagner's eyes in a disadvantageous light. Neither more nor less, they

* *Tannhäuser* was sung in French at the Opéra on March 13, 18, and 24, 1861. Disturbances created at its second and third performances by members of the Jockey Club insured its withdrawal from the boards.

pictured him as a false good fellow. I tried to enlighten Wagner on this subject and to tell him the exact truth.[18]

Rossini, no less annoyed, charged Liszt,

[18] I insisted above all that he should decide—with the aim of ending the persistence of these false rumors—to publish *in extenso* the account of what had occurred during his interview with Rossini; of the truly sympathetic welcome of which he had been the object; of the subjects, so full of interest, which had been broached during the course of their conversation . . . , etc. He refused. "What good would it do?" he answered. "With regard to what concerns his art and the way he practiced it, Rossini told me nothing more than his works demonstrate. On the other hand, if I report the exposition of my theories as I sketched them for him, that repetition would be as brief as it would be useless to the public, they being divulged sufficiently by my writings. Then there remains my appreciation of the man. Here, I confess to you, I was very much surprised to discover—if only in the way he talked to me about Bach and Beethoven—how much his intellect, nourished far more than I had believed on German art, showed itself to be superior. He grew swiftly in my estimation. Historically, the moment for judging him still has not arrived. He is in too good health and is too much in view as he walks about, the length of the Champs-Elysées (I have heard from those who meet him, all the way from the place de la Concorde to the Barrière de l'Étoile), for it to be possible to assign to him now the place that he will occupy among the masters, his predecessors and contemporaries who now walk, and forever, in the Elysian Fields of the other world." Wagner persisted in this view; one can detect it in the obituary article that he devoted to Rossini in 1869 [actually, 1868]. There he held himself to a very summary account of the 1860 interview.

among others, to invite Wagner to call upon him again so that he might furnish indisputable proofs of his entire innocence. Wagner declined that invitation, giving as his pretext that these pullulating tales would only increase from the moment when the press learned that he had called upon Rossini again; that these men had not as yet, in this regard, done anything but overlard their tittle-tattle with *Pater, peccavi;* that all this put him in a false position . . . that, furthermore, he kept himself from discussing Rossini further, never having veered away from the impression of profound sympathy for the nobility of his character which he [Wagner] had had since the first visit that he [Wagner] had paid him . . .

That was the end of the matter. He remained obdurate, though I unsuccessfully renewed a final invitation from Rossini, when he charged me with returning to Wagner's house the score of the "Graner" Mass which Liszt had lent to the Maestro.

I believe that the real reason for Wagner's refusal lay rather in his conviction that undertaking a second interview with the Italian master would profit him little. The purpose that he had proposed to himself when soliciting the first interview had, as I have explained, been achieved. He desired nothing further.

The two masters, then, never saw one another again; but I can certify that whenever Rossini's name came from Wagner's lips or pen, the latter never departed from the deference and profound esteem that he had conceived for him. It was the same with Rossini, who later on often asked me about what success Wagner's operas were meeting with in Germany, and regarding which he often charged me with transmitting to the latter his congratulations and remembrances.

An Evening at Rossini's in Beau-Sejour (Passy) 1858*

* The publication date of this pamphlet often is given as 1858, the date of the meeting it describes. But Michotte's mention in it of *Aida* "and its successors" among Verdi's operas makes certain that it was written later than 1893, as the *première* of *Falstaff*, the second—and last—"successor" to *Aida* occurred in that year.

[PASSY 1858]

Rossini's reputation for wit is universal. How has his public reputation not been abused—in the past, and even now—by thoughtless attribution to him of quantities of nonsense, of vacuous quips, of tasteless and sometimes malicious remarks having nothing whatever in common with the refined sallies, the humorous repartee, the mischievous mots of which the composer of *Il Barbiere* was prodigal? By himself, he had more wit than the multitude of anonymous people who labored to assign their own jokes to him.

When, feeling well and surrounded by his preferred friends, he found himself in his chosen milieu, his conversation was of an incomparable allure. What an abundance of memories, what a profusion of original ideas, of curious *aperçus*—not to mention the vivacity of his replies, his high-toned raillery, his unpredictableness—the words happily hit upon—the real pleasure in the charm of a picturesque way of speaking which was absolutely personal with him! [1]

In the following narrative—extracted from numerous notes that I have kept of intimate conversations—I have held to the purpose of integral transcription, of showing the reader a Rossini painted from life under circumstances in which, thanks to the presence of Alboni,* the Maestro improvised for us a detailed lecture on the principles followed in Italy in his time for teaching the great art of *bel canto* to the celebrated virtuosos of that era.

It was in Passy on a soft spring evening; Rossini [and Mme Rossini] had gathered around the

[1] He handled the French language perfectly, with the ease of a born Parisian. Furthermore, his second wife, Olympe Pélissier, was a Parisienne.

* Marietta Alboni (1823–1894) was one of the foremost contraltos of the 1840's, '50's, '60's, and '70's. An intimate friend of Rossini for some thirty years, she joined Adelina Patti in singing the *Quis est homo* from the *Stabat Mater* at his funeral in Paris on November 21, 1868. Her vocal range was extraordinary: it extended up from the G below the treble clef to the C above it; she sang soprano as well as contralto and mezzo-soprano roles.

table Mme Alboni, Prince Poniatowski,[2] Heugel,[3] Azévedo,[4] Scudo,[5] and the writer of this account.

We were taking coffee in the garden.

As was his habit after the evening meal, the Maestro lighted a cigar.

When taking it from a small box intended especially for that purpose, he said to Prince Poniatowski: "I don't offer you one of these cigars. They are so weak—the only ones, furthermore, that I can bear—that if were to give them to a corporal or, above all, to a sapper, they would both decamp *presto* rather than put themselves in a position of having to exhale such bland puffs."

This pleasant remark was a good omen, presaging mental treats of uncommon flavor for the rest of the evening.

He had spoken little during dinner, as usual, chewing having become a laborious process for him

[2] Senator, composer, creator of the opera *Pierre de Médicis.* [Prince Josef Poniatowski (1816–1873), a great-grandson of Stanislas II Augustus, King of Poland, was an operatic composer of some distinction and a long-time friend of Rossini.]

[3] The renowned publisher in the rue Vivienne. [Jacques-Léopold Heugel (1811–1883) took over the Meissonier music-publishing firm in 1812, changing its name to Heugel et Cie., as which it was active until 1940.]

[4] Music critic of *L'Opinion nationale.* [See translator's footnote, page 85.]

[5] Art critic of *La Revue des Deux-Mondes.* [Pierre Scudo (1806–1864), an opera singer turned journalist, was a leading reactionary music critic and a devoted Rossinian.]

after the disappearance of almost all of his teeth.[6]

We chatted on about this and that—about the news of the day . . . and precisely about Tamberlick's performances at the Théâtre-Italien. "On

[6] The time when the composer Carafa, a childhood friend, promised to have a set of false teeth made for him, citing himself as an example of their use. "Oh, you!" Rossini replied, "in your position as a professor of harmony, you have become familiar with substitutions with or without *appoggiature*, but I, I don't worry over them at all. As for my jaw, and how much of it is reflected in my music, I make fun of the others; furthermore, I don't like the *ut dièzes* [C-sharps].[1]

CARAFA: "The C-sharps?"

ROSSINI: "Look, when one is in the hands of dentists—those virtuosos of the gums—their *notes*—and I judge them from the metallic sounds that I hear emerging from my wife's purse [*bourse*], always are C-sharps."

[1] An allusion to the famous chest-tone C-sharp with which [Enrico] Tamberlik [the renowned tenor (1820–1889)] just then was attracting all Paris to the Théâtre-Italien in [Rossini's] *Otello*.

Rossini had a predilection for puns, particularly for those based on an allusion to musical terms. Example: one day he found [Luigi] Cherubini [(1760–1842), the distinguished composer and director of the Paris Conservatoire] in bed and complaining loudly of a *point de côté* [pain in the side]. "What nonsense!" Rossini exclaimed. "How nonsense?" the exasperated Cherubini replied. "Look, my physician, who just left here, is an ass and I, who am howling with pain, am a blockhead!" "Precisely, that's what I think. You, *you* can never have anything but a *contrepoint de côté* [counter-pain in the side, a pun on counterpoint]."

At these words, Cherubini was convulsed, not with pain, but with laughter.

that subject, Heugel," Rossini said. "I read in your *Ménéstrel* [*sic*] that at the performance of *Otello* the day before yesterday, after the explosion of the famous C-sharp, the audience seemed *transported* . . . *transported*, I suppose, by that excruciating shout, to an operating session in the maternity hospital. Oh, the ninnies!

"[Gilbert-Louis] Duprez * was the first one to think of chafing the Parisians' ears by disgorging in *Guillaume Tell* that chest-tone C of which I had never dreamed. [Adolphe] Nourrit ** had been satisfied with a head-tone C, which was what was required. Then, during my stay in Paris in 1837, *** just after Duprez's resounding debut in *Guillaume Tell*, the impetuous tenor came to see

* Duprez (1806–1896) made his Paris debut as Arnold in *Guillaume Tell* on April 17, 1837, and singlehandedly restored that opera to popularity, largely because of his unexampled chest-tone high C (he sang up to E in falsetto).

** Nourrit (1802–1839), who succeeded his father, Louis Nourrit, as leading tenor of the Paris Opéra, created four Rossinian roles: Néoclès in *Le Siège de Corinthe* (1826), Amenophis in *Moïse et Pharaon* (1827), Comte Ory in the opera of that name (1828), and Arnold in *Guillaume Tell* (1829), this last a part somewhat too high-lying and otherwise too difficult for him. He committed suicide at Naples when the censors there forbade the performance of *Poliuto*, an opera by Donizetti, who had designed its name role for him.

*** Rossini was not in Paris in 1837. His first visit to Paris after Duprez's sensational debut there in 1837 occurred in 1843—when the meeting with Duprez could have taken place.

me to invite me to hear him at the Opéra. "You come to see me instead," I told him. "You will produce your C for me alone, and I'll be more than flattered." I was staying with my friend [Eugène] Troupenas.* Duprez hastened to come. With Troupenas present, he sang for me—magnificently, I must admit—several fragments of my opera. At the approach of the '*Suivez-moi,*' ** I experienced the kind of anxious discomfort that some people feel when they know that a cannon is about to be shot off. Finally, he burst forth with the C! Zounds, what an uproar! I rose from the piano and rushed to a virtrine filled with very delicate Venetian glass which decorated Troupenas's salon. 'Nothing broken,' I exclaimed, 'That's wonderful!'

"Duprez appeared enchanted by my remark, which he took for a compliment in my style. 'Well, then, Maître, tell me sincerely, does my C please you?' 'Very sincerely, what pleases me most about your C is that it is over, and that I am no longer in danger of hearing it. I don't like unnatural effects. It strikes my Italian ear as having a strident timbre, like a capon squawking as its throat is slit. You are a

* Troupenas (1799–1850), a mathematician and intense music lover, began to publish music after inheriting a small fortune. He was a close friend of Rossini and the publisher of *Le Siège de Corinthe*, *Moïse et Pharaon*, *Le Comte Ory*, *Guillaume Tell*, and the *Stabat Mater*.

** In Arnold's "*Amis, amis.*"

very great artist, a true new creator of the role of Arnold. Why in the devil abase your talent by using that humbug?' 'Because,' Duprez answered, 'Opéra subscribers are accustomed to it now; that C is my great success . . .' 'Well, would you like an even greater success? Unload them two at a time.'

"Now comes Tamberlick. That jokester, wanting ardently to demolish Duprez's C, has invented the chest-tone C-sharp and loaded it onto me. In the finale of my *Otello* there is, in fact, an A that I emphasized. I thought that it, by itself, launched with full lungs, would be ferocious enough to satisfy the *amour-propre* of tenors for all time. But look at Tamberlick, who has transformed it into C-sharp, and all the snobs are delirious! Last week, he asked to come to see me. I received him. But, fearing a second, aggravated edition of the Duprez adventure, I cautioned Tamberlick please, when he came to see me, to deposit his C-sharp on the hall tree and pick it up again, guaranteed intact, when he left."

A great success for the amazing story of those celebrated C's, which the Maestro told calmly and with few gestures, in a manner brought on by age, but without the imprint of the years having affected his mental vivacity, more comical and more mischievous than ever.

When the conversation had turned more general, Alboni interrupted it by asking us if we knew "*L'Amour à Pekin,*" * one of the Maestro's recent compositions, which she had read through some days earlier.

Nothing more was needed to set tinder to the powder. We all asked for "*L'Amour à Pekin.*"

"Oh!" Rossini said. "It's a humbug."

* "*L'Amour à Pekin—Petite Mélodie sur la gamme chinoise*" is one of the *Péchés de vieillesse;* it appears in the *Album de morceaux réservés*, of which it is number 5; it has been recorded; it was published in *Quaderni Rossiniani*, V (Pesaro, 1956).

Nevertheless, the Maestro rose and led us into the salon without having to be begged excessively.

Sitting down at the piano and opening the manuscript: "I assure you," he repeated, "that it's nothing but a hoax on the notes of the Chinese scale, which is made up entirely of a series of tones without semitones.

and descending:

Needless to insist upon how Alboni, with her sumptuous voice, did justice to the piece.

I must confess, however, that the broad rhythm and the vocal qualities that mark the piece do not compensate for its lack of inspiration, which was hindered by the suppression of the semitones, the non-use of which dulls the expressive effect and is of a nature to engender monotony. Only details in the accompaniment and, above all, the succession of chords underlining the notes of the descending scale in the peroration, surprise by their harmonization, as piquant as it is unexpected.

The title "*L'Amour à Pekin*" provoked, in

that intimate circle, some very droll comments. "Well, what can one do?" Rossini replied in his bantering tone. "Whether it's in *Pé-Kin* or whether it's in *Kin*-Campoix,* love proceeds as loves always do, sharps in the prelude, flats in the coda."

Then Alboni sang "*L'Orpheline du Tyrol*," ** another of the maestro's recently hatched works. This really charming one was heard later during the soirées in the Chaussée d'Antin (Rossini's winter residence in Paris).

Because things were proceeding so well, Prince Poniatowski—and how right he was!—asked Alboni to sing the famous aria from *Semiramide*: "*Ah! quel giorno*," *** one of the eminent singer's triumphs.

"*Va bene!*" she exclaimed, running toward

---

* "*Kin*-Campoix" is pronounced exactly like Quincampoix, the name of a Paris street. A rough equivalent would be "Whether it's in Walla-Walla or Wall Street . . ."

** "*L'Orpheline du Tyrol*" is another of the *Péchés de vieillesse;* it appears in the *Album français,* of which it is number 11; it was published in *Quaderni Rossiniani,* V (Pesaro, 1956).

*** Arsace's *scena* (Act I, Scene 5) begins with the recitative "*Eccomi alfine in Babilonia,*" continues with the cavatina "*Ah! quel giorno ognor rammento,*" and culminates in the florid cabaletta "*Oh! come da quel dì tutto, tutto per me cangiò.*" Alboni was a foremost performer of the role of Arsace, which she often sang opposite Giulia Grisi.

Rossini, who had not risen from the piano. "*Benissime* for you, I'm sure," he told her, "but if you think that I can remember that old mummy dating from 1823 . . . the cavatina perhaps—but the rest . . . and the recitative?"

Astonishingly, the Maestro did not have copies of any of his early works in his home, not one of his forty operatic scores, whether in manuscript or as published.

When someone expressed astonishment over that fact, he answered: "And I, do you think that I'd be less astonished if you were to tell me that you had preserved, you, your old matchboxes and worn slippers?"

After a moment of reflection, the Maestro finally gave in to our insistence: "All right, so be it," he said to Alboni. "Let's attempt it. But all that I have retained of the recitative is the first words: "*Ecco mi al fine in Babilonia*." For the rest, you prompt me. So much the worse if I get mixed up. The devil will be to get to the cavatina without embarrassment. From that point on, I really hope to be able to save the rest."

Needless to say, everything went well.

How describe the unforgettable emotion that seized upon us while we were listening, perhaps for the last time, to that celebrated aria in all its splendid pomp and as only Alboni still had the style to interpret it, that model of vocal magnificence of which Garcia * said that "if all the vocal pieces of the Italian masters were to be destroyed, that aria would by itself suffice for reconstituting the entire art of *bel canto*"?

After the disappearance of the great virtuosos: the Nozzaris, Gallis, Davides, Rubinis,** and—among the female singers—the Colbrans, Pastas, Sontags, Pisaronis,*** and, most marvelous of them

* This could refer to either Manuel del Popolo Vicente Garcia (1775–1832), renowned tenor (the first Almaviva in *Il Barbiere di Siviglia*), composer, and singing teacher, or his son Manuel Patricio (1805–1906), one of the greatest of singing teachers.

** Andrea Nozzari (1775–1832), a tenor, created roles in nine of Rossini's operas. Filippo Galli (1783–1853), originally a tenor, became a notable *basso cantante* and created roles in eight of Rossini's operas and in Donizetti's *Anna Bolena*. Giacomo David(e) (1750–1830) was a leading tenor of the eighteenth century. His son Giovanni (1790–1864) was equally renowned in the nineteenth; he created roles in six of Rossini's operas. Giovanni Battista Rubini (1795–1854), regarded by many of his contemporaries as the finest tenor of his time, was noted for his assumption of many Rossinian and Donizettian roles.

*** Isabella Colbran (1786–1845) was Rossini's first wife; he shaped leading parts in ten of his Neapolitan operas for her. Giuditta Pasta (1799–1865), a foremost soprano of her time, appeared in the *première* of only one Rossinian opera (*Il Viaggio a Reims*, 1825), but sang with enormous success in most of the outstanding operas available to her. Henriette Sontag (1806–1854), a soprano, created the title role in Weber's *Euryanthe* and sang in the first performances of Beethoven's *Missa solemnis* and Ninth Symphony; she also all, the genius-gifted Malibran *—in a word, after that admirable school of which Alboni remains the final glory, our ears were not used to that masterly diction, to such solid *sostenuto* in that largo, with its lapidary structure "*Ah! quel giorno*," which ten cellos (Prince Poniatowski's remark was just) could not equal! I should add the impression made by the feverish vigor of the allegro: "*Oh! come da quel dì*," in which, despite the fast tempo of the writing and the multiplicity of notes, not one of them was slighted, not one but emerged without shock, without violence, in its full sonorous value!

When, borne away with admiration, we surrounded the great artist, Rossini became very animated and departed this time from the feigned or real indifference that he ordinarily displayed when, as he said, people made him "unpack one of his old things"—Rossini affectionately embraced his Marietta (he had known Alboni as a child at the Bologna Liceo and had been particularly involved

excelled in Italian opera. Benedetta Rosmunda Pisaroni (1793–1872), a contralto, created roles in three of Rossini's operas.

* Maria Malibran (1808–1836), daughter of Manuel del Popolo Vicente García, sister of Pauline Viardot-García and Manuel Patricio García, was one of the two or three greatest operatic singers of her era. She sang in several Rossini operas with clamorous success.

in her vocal education). Then he sighed: "*Ahi noi! perduto il bel canto della patria!* [Alas for us!—our homeland's *bel canto* is lost!]."

Then he added: "At present, with our so-called singers, *bel canto* is produced with a convulsive thrusting of the lips, from which there emerges, particularly with tenor-baritones, a tremolo that closely resembles the buzzing produced in my ears by the way the floor shakes at the approach of my brewer's chariot; whereas tenors and prime donne allow themselves—the former, vociferations, the latter, garglings [*gargouillades*], and these have in relation to REAL *vocalizations* and *roulades* nothing but the consonance of the rhymes."

Alboni added: "And the portamentos, which you haven't mentioned."

"Ah, yes! that plague," Rossini replied. "It had little place in my time. It happened, however, that the sorts of braying produced from top to bottom and the trumpetings loosed from bottom to top succeeded in astonishing the public's ears sometimes. Well, I advised the virtuosos of those eccentric mouthings to go and ask for bravos and recalls from the denizens of zoölogical gardens."

(We may presume that at the time these blows with the paw, as penetrating as they were intelligently conceived, referred to the interpreters of the operas—then much in vogue—of Verdi, the vocal form of which, the antipodes of the Rossinian style, had brought into style effects that were incorrect, harsh, and violent; and which con-

tributed brutally to hastening the rapid decay of the Italian school of *bel canto*. In that connection, Rossini was credited with a mot that the press hastened to spread; he was supposed to have said of Verdi: "He is a musician who wears a helmet." But the report was inexact; here is the truth. After reading one of Verdi's scores, the Maestro exclaimed: "If the name of the composer had been kept hidden from me, I should have wagered that he could only be an artillery colonel.") (I should add that at that time Verdi still had not written the scores of *Aida* and its successors.)

"Maestro," we demanded, "do you really believe that *bel canto* is irretrievably lost?"

"Absolutely," he answered sharply. "And at the beginning, let us understand what we mean by the term. Here, *bel canto* generally is confused with *fioriture*. That is a mistake. *Bel canto* is made up of three elements:

"1. The instrument—the voice—the *Stradivarius*, if you like;

"2. Technique—that is to say, the means of using it;

"3. *Style*, the ingredients of which are taste and feeling.

"Let's speak first of the voice, the instrument to be formed. Nature, alas, never creates all parts of a voice perfectly, any more than a pine tree gives birth to a *Stradivarius*. Just as an instrument maker must construct a Stradivarius, so it behooves a future singer to fabricate the instrument he counts upon using. And how long and arduous a labor that is!

"Among my compatriots, that job formerly was facilitated; in view of nature's refusal to comply, they made *castrati.* The method, to be sure, was heroic, but the results were wonderful. In my youth it was my good fortune still to be able to hear some of those fellows.

"I have never forgotten them. The purity, the miraculous flexibility of those voices and, above all, their profoundly penetrating accent—all that moved and fascinated me more than I can tell you. I should add that I myself wrote a role for one of them, one of the last but not of the least—Velluti.* That was in my opera *Aureliano in Palmira,* which was given in Milan in 1813.

"Would you believe, parenthetically, that I came within a hair's breadth of belonging to that famous corporation—let us, rather, say decorporation. As a child, I had a very pretty voice, and my parents used it to have me earn a few paoli by singing in churches. One uncle of mine, my mother's brother, a barber by trade,** had convinced my father of the opportunity that he had glimpsed if the breaking of my voice should not be

* Giovanni Battista (Giambattista) Vellutti (1780–1861) was a renowned soprano *castrato;* he was greatly admired in Vienna and London.

** Rossini's maternal uncle Francesco Maria Guidarini.

allowed to compromise an organ which—poor as we were, and I having shown *some* disposition toward music—could have become an assured future source of income for us all. Most of the *castrati*, and particularly those dedicated to a theatrical career, in fact lived in opulence. My brave mother would not consent at any price."

"And you, Maestro, the chief interested party?" Scudo asked.

"Oh! me," Rossini answered, "all that I can tell you is that I was very proud of my voice . . . And as for any descendants that I might leave . . ."

Mme Rossini interrupted: "Little you cared! Now is the moment for making one of your quips."

"Well, then, let's have no half-truths," the Maestro replied. " 'Little' is too much. I didn't care at all."

Then, after giving some details of the extraordinary virtuosity of the *castrati*, the Maestro went on in this way:

"Ah, yes, in those days the formation of the voice, the instrument, was an ungrateful labor.

"It began with work exclusively on the pure and simple emission of sound. Homogeneity of timbre, equalization of the registers—that was the basis of the apprenticeship upon which all later study was based. That practical instruction filled up at least three years of exercises.

"When I went back to stay in Bologna after abandoning my theatrical career, I was entirely

taken up with the teaching of singing at the Liceo. I just mentioned homogeneity of timbre, equalization of the registers. Here, for example, is a model of the exercises that I prescribed, thanks to which I obtained astonishing results. It is simple, and the pupil himself, given a good ear, came to be able to correct himself." Then, sitting down at the piano, the Maestro struck the following notes:

"After which the same exercise was continued through ascending semitones C-C-sharp, D-D-sharp, E, etc., to the limit of the voice's tessitura, variable according to age and to the progress of the martyr or *victim*," Rossini said, exchanging a smile with his illustrious former pupil Alboni.

"Without that first discipline, aimed at developing equality of timbre over the whole range of the organ, a voice, no matter how richly endowed by nature it may be, always will remain completely defective. Isn't that the case, what's more, with the brain, the most generous innate capacities of which demand long, studious effort if they are to acquire their full value?"

Then, continuing his demonstration: "Upon certain pupils, whose emission was functionally faulty, often as the result of a not very appropriate development of the voice, the teacher imposed special gymnastics of guttural contractions that the patient, I must say, had to practice without emitting the tiniest sound; that purely aphonic gymnastic could go on for months and months.

"When the voice finally had acquired the desired suppleness and equality—that is to say, when the future singer was in possession of his Stradivarius—only then did he begin to learn *the way to use* it! THE TECHNIQUE, which included placement, the holding of sound, and all the exercises in virtuosity: *vocalises, gruppetti*, trills, etc."

Alboni interrupted. "For three years, my teacher kept me at a single page, which I still have, and which includes by itself all the types of scholastic exercises for holding, agility, etc."

"And which taught you," Rossini added, "to construct the sound somewhat differently from today's practice; for now the would-be singers are, we must agree, peculiar apostles. Whereas a long apprenticeship is necessary in order to play the clarinet, an instrument that is *already made*, these singers, vainly confident about an instrument that has not yet been made at all—that is, a worn, unequal, badly placed voice—approach the public without wincing, all the while not knowing how to tame a note without repeating it in some way, nor how to let it die out naturally without a glottal stroke with the quality of an aborted hiccough.

"And there you have the miscarriages over which present-day snobbism swoons! *Miseria!*

"If I have spoken only of male singers," the Maestro added with a sly air, "don't think that I shall plait wreathes for the ladies. On the contrary!"

Then he went on: "After that, the work with the vowels began. Here is what that consisted of: the placement of the sounds and the *vocalises* were practiced from the first on the vowels, one at a time, a, e, i, o, u; then all five of them were produced alternatively on the same held tone or the same figure.

"For example:

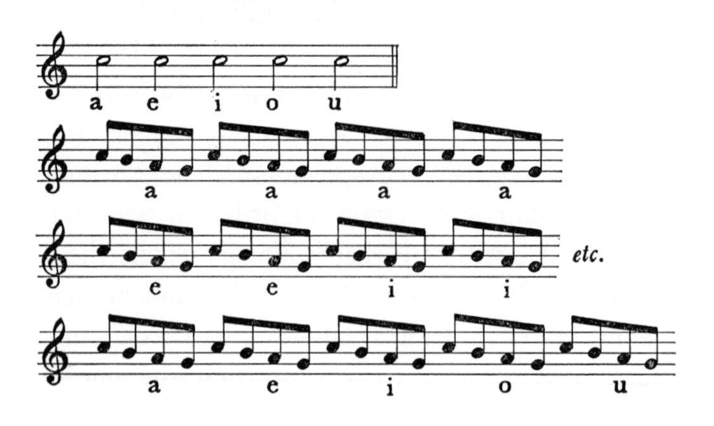

"This system was practiced on all the sustained tones and through all the exercises, which were complicated to infinity.

"The aim was to reach the point at which, as much as possible, the sound would not vary in timbre or intensity in spite of movements of the tongue and displacements of the lips caused by the succession of vowels, sometimes open, sometimes closed. In that way, one obtained o's that did not seem to have come from a megaphone, e's that did not resemble the noise of a rattle, and i's that were not mixed *à la vinaigrette.** That was one of the subtlest parts of the teaching.

"The study of the vowels was followed by that of the diphthongs, consonants, articulation, breathing, etc. Special attention was paid, above all, to the sound created with the help of the roof of the mouth. In fact, it is the transmitter *par excellence* of beautiful sounds. And in that regard one must agree that the Italian language really seems privileged to favor the evolution of *bel canto. Amâre . . . bêllo . . .* Those *mâ*s and *bêll*s, placed in the roof of the mouth and sounded thus—isn't that already a sort of music?

"A student showing any tendency to roll his

* It should be kept in mind that in both Italian and French the vowel *e* has something the sound of the English interjection *eh*, *i* that of the long English *e* (as in *see*).

r's, to lisp, to quaver, or to spice his emission with a dash of the guttural would have been singled out as a dangerous being liable to banishment if he remained impervious to correction. As for such as trumpeted through their noses, the teacher ordinarily advised them to enroll in a fanfare corps."[7]

[7] He sometimes gave the most laughable characterizations of some of these defects:

To a person who sang a cavatina for him in an obstinately guttural manner: "There's a cavatina," he said, "that seems to be coming out of a cave. You must know that caves are said to produce good mushrooms? Frankly, I'd have preferred a plate of that sort."

A friend had asked him to agree to hear a young tenor; unhappily, the man rolled his r's terribly. Suddenly the Maestro, who was at the piano, stopped playing, turned aside, and said: "Where, then did you get the habit of winding your watch while singing?"

A baritone much in favor with the public had sought the privilege of singing for the Maestro. He had talent; but—a fault commoner than you might believe—he made the succeeding word wait more or less upon the note. "A beautiful voice," Rossini said, "but you have a case of syllabic constipation. You must take care of that."

A not unpicturesque remark about an obese lady singer whose mouth had all but vanished in an incredible mass of fat. The unfortunate woman stammered outrageously as a result of that superabundant generosity on nature's part. "That's what you might call singing *properly*," Rossini said. "Each note creates the effect of having escaped from a tub of lard."

One day he was asked by his barber to examine the man's son, who was reputed to possess an unparalleled voice. In fact, it was a thunderous organ of rare species. Unhappily, nature also had given the fellow a roughness that the Mae-

"The third phase of the training consisted of putting into practice as a whole everything that had been studied in detail over a period of not less than five years for girls, seven for men. Then, at the end of a final year, the teacher could say proudly to that student—who had scarcely tried out a cavatina in class: 'Go now, get on with you. You can sing whatever you wish.'

"That is the truth. He was capable of singing anything. And nevertheless, something remained for him to learn; that something without which the most accomplished virtuosity, even when it bears the imprimatur of many awards won in the Liceo, still remains in some way comparable to an or-

---

stro compared to a steel file. "Under these circumstances," he said, "that is an irremediable vice. But don't take it too hard. Your son has many resources for becoming a commander of zouaves, a barricade chief, an animal tamer—or, above all, the times being what they are, a first-prize winner at the Conservatoire."

A friend who was a good musician wrote him from Dieppe: "There is a young girl here who has an admirable voice. She has only one dream, which is for you to hear her. If you agree, she will leave for Paris at once, accompanied by her mother. I believe that she has a fortune in her throat." The Maestro responded: "Given that that's the way it is, dissuade these ladies from making the trip to Paris. But persuade them to go to a surgeon as soon as possible so that he can extract *prestissimo* from that phenomenal throat the fortune that it contains. Can one ever be certain of the future? A bird in the hand is worth two in the bush!"

And so on without end.

ganism full of latent life but awaiting a ray of warm sunlight to transform itself into movement, strength, magnificence, and seductiveness.

"That warm ray—it is *style*. Style is traditions, and the secrets of those traditions could be surprised by the young novice only among great singers, the perfect models consecrated by fame.

"Those traditions, on the other hand, elude scholastic instruction. Only the *performing model*, taken from life, can inculcate and transmit them. So that if those who possess the great, true traditions disappear without leaving disciples on their level, their art vanishes, dies. *De profundis!* . . . In my time, there were numerous incomparable virtuosos in whose presence the new adepts could initiate themselves into taste, elegance, the judicious use of all the vocal effects—into *style*, that is.

"As for the qualities of expression, feeling, grace, charm, stage insight: that is an affair of the individual temperament.

"Let's finish, then: today there is no such school, there are neither models nor interpreters, for which reason not a single voice of the new generation is capable of rendering in *bel canto* the aria '*Casta Diva*' [8] or '*Pria che spunti*'; [9] or any

[8] From Bellini's *Norma*.

[9] From Cimarosa's *Il Matrimonio segreto*.

other you like—how can you imagine that it is possible to resuscitate what is dead, what is less than a mummy?

"What genius, be he more perspicacious than a Champollion,* could succeed in reconstituting that which has no tradition but oral tradition—let us rather say vocal tradition? And then, a parallel phenomenon will suggest itself: whence and by what miracle will disciples appear who, in our times, will consent to submit to the long, severe regimen that I just detailed?

"The railroads, a devilish invention, have unsettled everything—not to mention the formidable currents of international air, the permanent breathing of which, as they blow through those multiple tunnels of Hell, finally will give all humanity a cold—has instilled into the present generation the need to get things done quickly, the fever to arrive. The theaters pullulate; the impresarios, who are legion, carve arrows out of any kind of wood. And behold! . . . Here, for example, my concierge's daughter. She is eighteen, and she aspires to learn singing so as to go into the theater. One won't ever be able to remove from her head the idea that at the end of one year she will be arch-capable of making a debut in *Les Hugue-*

* Jean-François Champollion (1790–1832) worked out, from study of the Rosetta stone, the secret of deciphering Egyptian hieroglyphics.

nots!" * With his mischievous air, Rossini added: "Who would dare assert that she won't become a celebrity as a result, a Patti,** a star to be cited as a model of perfection? At the present time, that's not so difficult!"

"Speaking of Patti, whose name you just mentioned," Heugel interrupted, "what, dear Maître, is your final opinion of her talent?"

"My opinion is that she is charming and that I love her very much."

"And then? . . ."

"And then . . . that fate has been very gallant toward her in protecting her from the danger of being contemporary with, for example, Sontag . . . not to cite others."

"Which means," Azevedo answered, "that today, lacking thrushes, we must content ourselves with blackbirds."

Rossini said nothing more. A significant pause.

"Well," we said, "with you, Maestro, it is necessary, then, to repeat in chorus: '*De profundis il bel canto*?' "

"Certainly," Rossini added, "one still encoun-

* Opera by Giacomo Meyerbeer.

** Adelina Patti (1843–1919), one of the most agile and popular of operatic sopranos and a friend of Rossini. She made her official debut, as Lucia di Lammermoor, in New York on November 24, 1859, when only sixteen.

ters singers who are thoroughbreds, really great singers who apply the highest qualities of dramatic expression, of theatrical understanding, to interpreting—supposing that their imperfect vocal techniques will still permit it—the roles that were made to be sung by the masters who in their time wrote for *the voice that sings*. As for the composers who write for *the voice that does not sing*, would you call their interpreters singers?

"That would be like calling laborers the nomads who cross the desert sand trying to collect a few blades of grass there. But, truly, such great singers as Nozzari, Davide, Garcia, Rubini . . . and admirable ladies like Marcolini,* Colbran, Pasta, Sontag, and Malibran—I cite only a few names among the vanished glories representing the divine art of song at perfection—they will appear no more . . . unless it should be the aforementioned daughter of my concierge!"

Amid the laughter evoked by this last sally:

"And among the elite lady singers whom you have just enumerated, Maestro, which—we ask you—do you judge to have been the greatest?"

"The greatest was *Colbran*, who became my first wife, but the *unique* was *Malibran*. Ah! that

* Maria Marcolini (1780–?), a contralto, was especially noted for her comic roles. She created parts in five of Rossini's operas.

marvelous creature! She surpassed all her imitators by her truly disconcerting musical genius, and all the women I have ever known by the superiority of her intelligence, the variety of her knowledge,

and her flashing temperament, of which it is impossible to give any idea. Knowing the most diverse languages, she sang in Spanish (her native tongue), Italian, French, German, and after eight days of study, she sang *Fidelio* in English in London. She sketched, painted, embroidered, sometimes made her own costumes; above all, she wrote. Her letters are masterpieces of subtle intelligence, of verve, of good humor, and they display unparalleled originality of expression.

"In that connection, I'll tell you about an event that, under Malibran's influence, later resulted in a very curious change in my habits. At the time when I was composing, I refused to put my foot inside the theater again to hear an opera once the rehearsals were over. An exception, however; but one I was forced to by contract. I had conducted the *première* of *Il Barbiere* at Rome. The work fell flat. Coming out of the theater by a secret door, I was recognized, unfortunately; an angry mob, with raised fists, pursued me with such rage, mixed with hisses, whoops, and even projectiles, that I thought that the end of my existence had come.

"You here, you have not the least notion of the excesses of which the descendants of the gentle Numa Pompilius * are capable when, gathered in a theater to attend the *première* of a new work, they decide that they are not getting their money's worth. They inflict upon the unhappy author the severest punishment, for which one can only pity him. Me, I had been punished by the ruining of a handsome new jacket with gold buttons which I had had made for me at the expense of my poor

* A legendary Sabine king of Rome (715–673 B.C.).

purse so that I might look decent on the conductor's podium. That unhappy jacket, which was of a hazel color, was ruined by the filth with which it had been covered during the uproar. I asked the servant at my hotel to accept it as it was—naturally, after I had removed the gold buttons, which were worth thirty francs."

"A relic which, if it could be found again," Prince Poniatowski exclaimed, "would not, in its pacific way, be out of place alongside the terrible gray cloak." *

"However, Maestro, one must add," Azevedo said, "that you were vindicated triumphantly the next day, when the same Romans, coming from the second performance of *Il Barbiere*, arrived in a crowd to give you an ovation."

"Stop!" Rossini said. "You are reminding me of the greatest fright that I ever felt in my life. I was peacefully sleeping when I was awakened suddenly by a deafening uproar in the street, accompanied by a bright glow of torches which I saw approaching the hotel as soon as I got up. Still half asleep, and recalling the scene of the preceding night, I thought that they were coming to set fire to the building, and so I took the precaution of going to a stable at the back of the courtyard. But behold, after a few instants I hear García calling me at the

* Apparently a reference to Napoleon's "*terrible capote gris.*"

top of his voice. He finally found me. 'Get a move on you; come now; hear those shouts of *bravo, bravissimo Figaro*. An unprecedented success. The street is full of people; they want to see you.' 'Tell them,' I answered—still having at heart the fact that my new jacket had gone to the devil, 'that I f . . . them, their bravos, and all the rest. I'm not coming out of here.' I don't know how poor García presented my refusal to that turbulent crowd—in fact, he was struck in the eye by an orange, tumefied traces of which formed a black circle visible for several days. Meanwhile, the uproar in the street increased more and more . . . The proprietor of the hotel arrived in turn, breathless: 'If you don't come out, they'll set fire to my building; now they're breaking windows . . .' 'That's your affair,' I told him, 'you have only to avoid standing behind your windows . . . Me, I'm staying where I am.' Finally I heard panes of glass crashing. Then, war-weary, the crowd finally dispersed. I left my refuge and went back to bed. Unhappily, the brigands had defenestrated two windows facing the bed. It was January.* I should be lying if I told you that the icy air coming into my room gave me a delicious night!

"The next morning, the hotel keeper came to tell me that the loss he had suffered in fifteen bro-

* The date was actually February 22, 1816.

ken windows was entirely a result of my stubbornness, and that he had the right to put the costs on my bill, but that he wouldn't do anything if I would agree to get out of his hotel within twenty-four hours. Entirely in accord with him about that very agreeable project, I installed myself in the diligence leaving for Naples the next day. All the interpreters of my *Barbiere*, hearing about my precipitous departure, came to bid me farewell. I was touched most by the visit of García, my incomparable *Almaviva*, accompanied by his eight-year-old daughter, the future Malibran! As soon as she came in, she bounded toward me and, dissolved in tears, clung to my neck, crying: 'Ah! if mama only had sent me to the theater last night!'

" 'And what would you have done?'

" 'Oh, while they were hissing your beautiful music, I should have shouted with all my strength: "You are all snakes; go back to the wild places and understand the music of the bears, the only sort that you deserve!" '

"She really would have been capable of doing just that," Rossini added, "for she was a little demon. Then she said to me: 'Don't be sad: listen: when I am grown up, I'll sing *Il Barbiere* everywhere, but (tapping her foot) never at *Rome*, even if the Pope on both knees begs me to.'

"When the visit was over, she was still throwing me from the door a quantity of kisses from her little hands, and she went away singing '*Una voce poco fa.*' Would you believe that that *gamine*, after attending only a few rehearsals of *Il Barbiere*, had remembered nearly all of the pieces?"

The Maestro went back to his story: "I said then that once the rehearsals were over, it was my custom never to attend a performance of any of my operas. That surprises you? Frankly, what would have been the sense of my wasting my time in order to find out how I had written them?"

"It even seems," Scudo observed, "that you have never been to a single performance of *Guillaume Tell* at the Opéra."

"That is true. The singers came to rehearse at my place—I was living in the boulevard Montmartre, above the passage Jouffroy. After hearing two complete rehearsals in succession, though without the stage costumes, I had had enough. Until—and now I return to my subject—it was a question of performances with Malibran. That was something else. When she was to appear in *Semiramide*, *La Gazza ladra*, *Cenerentola*, *Il Barbiere*, above all in *Otello*, nothing could have kept me from going to hear her. The fact was that each time her creative genius inspired her in a stupefying, always different way with unexpected effects, both vocal and declamatory . . . Each time, too, she taught me how I could have done *better* than I had done."

The conversation continued merrily. Scudo,

who at the time was busy on a history of the Théâtre-Italien, said: "Maître, a few moments ago you mentioned the names of admirable virtuosos who graced the era of your youth. What comparison would you make between them and their successors, the ones whose undeniable talent continues today to maintain the glory of the Italian schools—such as Mario, Gardoni, Zucchini, Badiali, Tamburini * . . . and, among the women, Frezzolini, Grisi, Bosio, Borghi-Mamo,** etc?

* Mario, Cavaliere di Candia (1810–1883), a tenor, made his operatic debut in Meyerbeer's *Robert le Diable* at the Paris Opéra in 1838; he retired in 1867 after a very successful career; he married Giulia Grisi. Italo Gardoni (1821–1882), a tenor, sang successfully from 1840 to about 1870; he created a role in Verdi's London opera, *I Masnadieri.* Giovanni Zucchini (1812–1892), a *buffo* baritone, was a leading singer from about 1848 to 1884; he was particularly admired in *Il Barbiere di Siviglia* and Donizetti's *Don Pasquale.* Cesare Badiali (1810?–1865), a bass, made his operatic debut when very young; he sang to acclaim in operas by Rossini, Donizetti, and Verdi; in 1842, he sang in Rossini's *Stabat Mater* at Vienna under Donizetti's direction. Antonio Tamburini (1800–1876), a bass-baritone, was one of the foremost operatic singers of his era; he created roles in almost a dozen of Donizetti's operas (he was the first Malatesta in *Don Pasquale*).

** Erminia Frezzolini (1820–1884), a daughter of the noted *basso buffo* Giuseppe Frezzolini and wife of the tenor Antonio Poggi, became a much-appreciated operatic soprano; she created the role of Giselda in Verdi's *I Lombardi alla prima crociata* (1843). Giulia Grisi, a niece of the renowned contralto Giuseppina Grassini, a sister of the mezzo-soprano Giuditta Grisi, and a cousin of the singer

"Naturally, I do not mention our Alboni or Lablache,* both of whom are unequaled."

"Certainly," Rossini replied, "their technical education was not subjected to the severe, long-applied principles of which I gave you a brief sketch; but some part of the good tradition has remained familiar to them. There are still stars of a beautiful grandeur. But it soon will be difficult to find among the reputations now in vogue, Faure ** excepted, newly emerged models worthy

---

Ernesta Grisi (Mme Théophile Gautier) and the great ballerina Carlotta Grisi, married as her second husband the tenor known as Mario. She shared the general repertoire of her foremost "rivals": Giuditta Pasta, Maria Malibran, and Henriette Sontag. Angiolina Bosio (1830–1859) made her debut at Milan in 1846 in Verdi's *I Due Foscari.* Becoming internationally famous as a soprano, she visited Havana, New York, Philadelphia, and Boston—and died in a carriage en route from Moscow to St. Petersburg. Adelaide Borghi-Mamo (1829–1901), a noted contralto (her daughter Erminia later became a noted soprano), was famed for her roles in operas by Rossini, Donizetti, and Verdi.

* Luigi Lablache (1794–1858), born in Naples of French parents, became the foremost *basso buffo* of his time and one of its leading *bassi cantanti.* He created roles in Bellini's *I Puritani di Scozia* (1835), Donizetti's *Marino Faliero* (1835) and (title role) *Don Pasquale* (1843), and (opposite Jenny Lind) Verdi's *I Masnadieri* (1847).

** Jean-Baptiste Faure (1830–1914), the foremost French bass-baritone of his time, created many roles, including Nelusko in Meyerbeer's *L'Africaine* (1865), Rodrigo in Verdi's *Don Carlos* (1867), and the title role in Ambroise Thomas's *Hamlet* (1868). He was a renowned Méphistophélès in Gounod's *Faust;* he is also remembered as the composer of the song "Les Rameaux."

of comparison to them. Alas! time, the oblit-erator, gradually will close in over these latter. After which, a few rare nebulae still, here and there . . . Then, no more . . . the final night."

"In the meantime"—it was the voice of Mme Rossini—"another sort of night had arrived, announced by the clock. It is ten o'clock."

"The canonical hour" (the Maestro's phrase for his invariable retiring time).

"Then, *messieurs*" [Mme Rossini said], "I shall take you all to the door. You must see that this evening you have subtly *emptied* my husband again. You are unbearable friends, examining magistrates; won't your interrogations ever come to an end?"

"Never! Madame . . . insatiable like treasure hunters!" Azevedo replied.

That was the final word.

Buona sera. To Alboni, who went up to embrace him: "*Buona sera, l'ultima diva del mio cuore* [Good night, final *diva* of my heart]."

That is a specimen of one of the numerous conversations in which, as we have just seen, having a place in which to enjoy himself when surrounded by a circle of intimate friends, the Maestro minced no words. During the gala soirées in the Chaussée d'Antin, on the other hand, where a crowd always gathered, he did not open his mouth.

Appendix

(BY THE TRANSLATOR)

Eduard Hanslick's Visits to Rossini in 1860 and 1867

Emil Naumann's Visit to Rossini in 1867

SHORTLY after Wagner's call at Rossini's Paris home, the distinguished Viennese critic Eduard Hanslick (1825–1904), perhaps the leading anti-Wagnerian (he is caricatured in *Die Meistersinger von Nürnberg* as Sixtus Beckmesser), visited Rossini. In an article entitled "Musical Recollections of Paris (1860)," included in his *Aus dem Concert-Saal* (Vienna, 1897 edition), Hanslick wrote of Rossini:

"Great musical controversies and turning points, as for example *Zukunftsmusik* [the Wagner-Liszt "music of the future"], have no interest beyond curiosity for the composer of *Il Barbiere.* A year ago Rossini took the baths at Kissingen. When he appeared in the pump room, the orchestra at once played selections from his operas. 'You can scarcely imagine how boring that was for me. I thanked the conductor and told him that I'd much rather hear something that I didn't know, something by Richard Wagner, for example.' He then heard the *Tannhäuser* March, which he quite liked, and another piece that he could no longer recall; that's all that he knew of Wagner. Rossini wanted to know something about the story of *Lohengrin.* After I had explained it as briefly and clearly as possible, he exclaimed gaily in his funny accent: '*Ah, je comprends! c'est un Garibaldi qui s'en va aux nues!* [Ah, I see, it's a Garibaldi who's taken up into the clouds].' Richard Wagner, who had visited the old gentleman recently, 'didn't seem at all like a revolutionary'; anyone who knows that dainty little man, that untiring and witty conversationalist, will gladly agree with that. Wagner, Rossini continued, introduced himself immediately with the quieting assurance that he had not the slightest intention of overthrowing existing music as people said he had. 'Dear sir,' Rossini interrupts him, 'that's of no importance at all; if your revolution succeeds, then you were absolutely right; if you don't succeed, then, with or without revolution, you miscalculated.' Rossini did not want to hear anything about a mischievous joke then circulating in Paris which compared Wagner's music to 'fish sauce without fish'; I would have believed him completely if he had not added in his droll, solemn manner: '*Je ne dis jamais de telles choses* [I never say such things].' Well, one knows so many and such clever '*de telles choses*' by Rossini that his inclination to irony is utterly beyond doubt. In that vein, he is credited with having exclaimed recently, after looking through a Berlioz score, 'How fortunate that this is not music!' "

More than seven years later, Hanslick wrote, in one of his "Musical Letters from Paris" (July 18, 1867, in the 1897 Vienna edition of *Aus dem Concert-Saal*), of a second call upon Rossini, who by then was seventy-five years old. Suddenly Rossini had asked whether or not the Beethoven monument in Vienna had been completed. " 'I remember Beethoven very well,' Rossini went on after a brief pause, 'though it will soon be half a century. During my stay in Vienna, I hastened to seek him out.'—'And, as [Anton Felix] Schindler * and other biographers assure us, he didn't admit you.'—'On the contrary,' Rossini corrected me, 'I

* Schindler (1795–1864) for a time served as Beethoven's friendly secretary. His *Biographie Ludwig van Beethovens* was published at Münster in 1840.

had asked the Italian poet Carpani, with whom I had visited Salieri earlier, to introduce me to Beethoven, who received us at once, and very politely. Of course, the visit didn't last very long, as conversation with Beethoven really was painful. He was hearing especially badly that day, and though I spoke as loudly as possible, he didn't understand me; furthermore, his lack of facility in Italian may have made the conversation even more difficult for him.' I confess that this information, the truth of which was corroborated by numerous details, pleased me like an unexpected gift. I always had been irritated by this incident in Beethoven's life, as well as by those musical Jacobins who had glorified the brutal German virtue of denying admittance to a Rossini. Well, the whole story was false.* Another example of the unconcern with which incorrect data are presented and repeated so that they can harden into historic truth at an incredible rate. And all that while it still would be so easy to obtain authentic enlightenment from living participants!"

About three months before Hanslick's 1867 visit to Rossini, Emil Naumann (1827–1888), Ger-

* This fictitious account of Beethoven's rudeness to Rossini nonetheless was repeated in several biographies of Beethoven, including that by Wilhelm Joseph von Wasielewski (*Beethoven*, 2 vols., 1888).

man composer and writer, had called on the elderly Italian. In his 1876 book *Italienische Tondichter, von Palestrina bis auf die Gegenwart*, Naumann wrote:

"Suddenly he [Rossini] interrupted himself with the words: '*A propos*, how is Monsieur Richard Wagner? Is he still the idol of Germany, or has the fever with which he infected your compatriots subsided? But, wait a moment—I am so thoughtless—perhaps you yourself are a Wagnerian, and if so perhaps you don't think that you and the other German are plagued by a fever, but rather that the one who is is I, the old man?' I assured him that he need not worry in that respect, my ideals being our great classical composers; nevertheless, I could not refrain from declaring that, Mendelssohn, Robert Schumann, and Meyerbeer now being dead, Richard Wagner was the most significant and independent talent among living German composers.—'Oh, in that respect, I completely agree with you,' Rossini exclaimed, 'and nothing could be farther from my mind than doubting the originality of the creator of *Lohengrin;* but occasionally the composer makes it very hard for us to find the beauties for which we are indebted to him amid the chaos of sounds that his operas contain. You will have experienced that yourself: *Monsieur Wagner a de beaux moments*, *mais de mauvais quart-d'heures!* [Monsieur Wagner has beautiful moments, but bad longueurs]! There is only one thing that I never understood and still cannot understand: how it is possible for a people that has produced a Mozart ever to begin to forget him because of a Wagner!' "

Index

Index

Index

Index